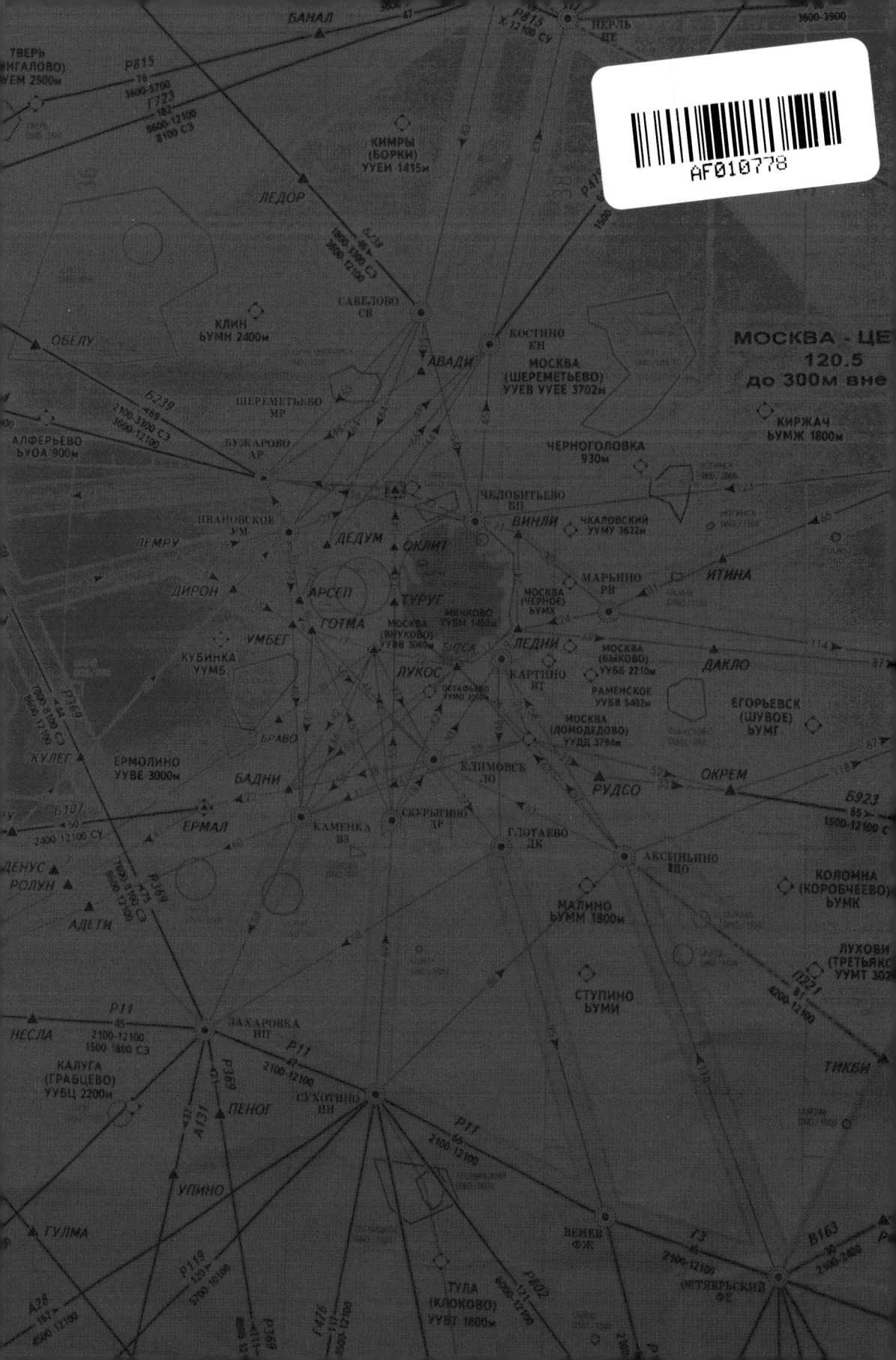

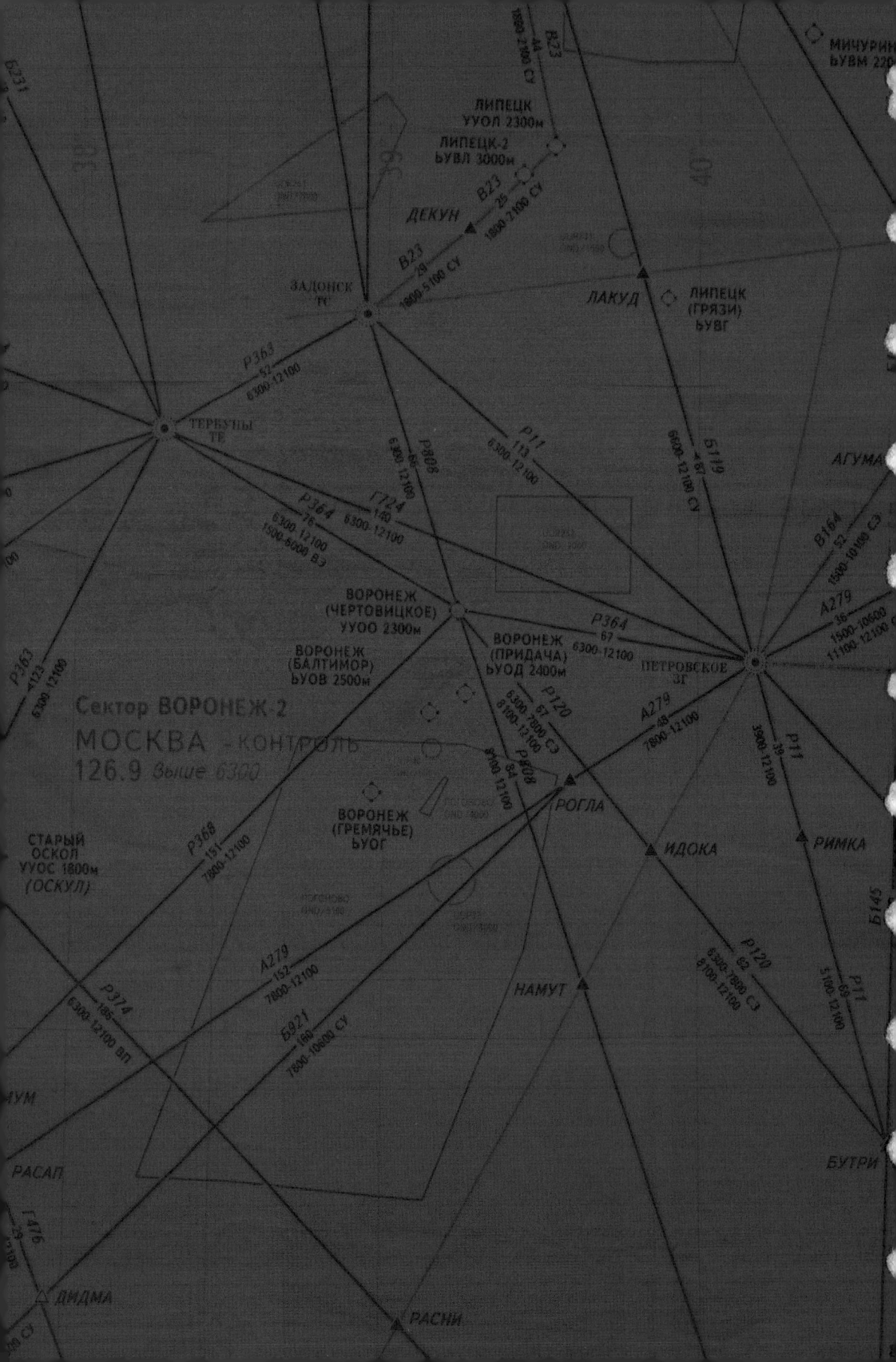

Jetliners of the Red Star

Charles Kennedy

Designed by Simon De Rudder

Jetliners Of The Red Star
978-1-9160396-0-5
Third edition, 2020
Copyright © 2018 Astral Horizon Press
All rights reserved

Astral Horizon Press
www.astralhorizon.co.uk
www.theairlineboutique.com

Design by Simon De Rudder
Printed in The Netherlands

Большому кораблю - большое плавание
For a big ship, a big voyage

The author would like to thank
Bhavna Vader, Emma Entero, Steve Finnigan and all at Astral Horizon Press and The Airline Boutique for making this book possible, Invisible Hands Music, and the Mortimer Street Gang - Scarlett Daisy Stansell, James Barker, Liv Slania and Neo, Jim Green, Tom Pearce, Aira Bekeryte, Graham Stokes, Nick Fleming, Sean Cooney, Ryan Nisley

Jonathon Falconer at Haynes; Craig West, James Ronayne, Andy Martin and Barry Woods-Turner at Airliner World; Dino Carrara at Aviation News; Andy Mason at Key Publishing; Enrique Perella at Airways – for publishing my writing

Guy Van Herbruggen, Torbjorn "Banjo" Okland, Manuel Kliese, Sam Chui, Shahram "Shary" Sharifi, Rob Reynolds, Leonid Faerberg, Artyom Kuzhlev, Lesley Turner, Susan Roller, Charles Gowlland, Jeremy Major, Phoenix Anthony Robins, Julian Nowill, Dave Bolger, France Maria and José Van Herbruggen, Cody Diamond and Jannik Femerling in the Time Capsule To Paradise, Matthew Murray, Geonelle Rose, Louis Barfe, Stevie Babes Thorpe, Will Wadhams, and all at the Flying Tiger Line Pilots Association (and in particular John Dickson and Rudi Kohlbacher)

Wing commanders Peter Shorter, Peter Preston, MigBro Chris Belcher and Matt Rigby for getting me airborne; Captain Adrian Potter, Captain Paul Bradd, Captain Ian Rowell, Senior First Officer Michael Plock; and notable Charlie Airlines passengers Edward Crossing, Camille Kapoor, Tony and Lee Boden, Lucy Hickman, Tim Gebbett, Sean Burris, Emily Jane Brown, and Harriet Palmer-Sands

Philipp Schaer at MigFlug, who have made it possible to add some truly incredible aircraft to my pilots logbook, including a MiG-15; check out MigFlug.com

Juche Travel Services commander David Thompson-Rowlands, fellow JTS guides Ben Griffin and James Scullin, and the Korea International Travel Company in Pyongyang; single hearted unity

British Airways, who do a fantastic job of getting me out on the road and back home in style every time, and Alrosa Airlines for an unforgettable Tu-154 jumpseat ride back from Baikonour to Moscow

Big smile and a wave for lovely family - Lucy Edward Alice and Rob Crossing, Donald Kennedy, Fiona Alan Felicity Rebecca and Elliot Weal, Kylie Evie and Michael Patrick, Robert Grant, Edwina Grant Tony and Asha, Kate and San Sri, Sally and Matt Montgomery, Angus Grant

Soundtrack to writing: Mew, Tangerine Dream, Gary Numan, Laaraji, The Midnight, "My Life In The Bush Of Ghosts" by Brian Eno and David Byrne, "Soul Of The Machine" by Windham Hill, Leroy Hutson, Brazilectro Session 7, Fairuz, The Avalanches, Clogs, Philip Glass, Harold Budd

Dedicated to my mum, Sally Grant Kennedy -- forever in our hearts.

5	**Jetliners Of The Red Star**	Air travel in the Soviet Union
17	**Tupolev Tu-104 & -124**	The start of the art
29	**Tupolev Tu-134**	The fighter jet
47	**Ilyushin Il-62**	The flagship
63	**Tupolev Tu-144**	The Soviet SST
77	**Tupolev Tu-154**	The workhorse
99	**Yakovlev Yak-40 & -42**	The unsung heroes
115	**Ilyushin Il-86 & -96**	The peoplemovers
135	**Tupolev Tu-204 & -214**	The bridge to the future
149	**Aeroflot timetable**	winter 1985 / 1986

Cover photo by B. Korzin Transport-Photo Images
Title page photo by Mark J Nutter

Valentin Grebnev Transport-Photo Images

Jetliners Of The Red Star

The Union Of Soviet Socialist Republics, more commonly known as the Soviet Union, was the biggest country the world has ever seen, covering a sixth of Earth's surface area and spanning eleven times zones. It measured 10,000 kilometres (6,200 miles) from east to west and 7,200 kilometres (4,500 miles) from north to south. Its border stretched more than 60,000 kilometres (37,000 miles), two thirds of which was coastline. The rest was a land border with Afghanistan, China, Czechoslovakia, Finland, Hungary, Iran, Mongolia, North Korea, Norway, Poland, Romania and Turkey.

Forged by the red heat of two socialist revolutions in 1917 that saw the abolition of the Romanov monarchy in Russia, and formally established in December 1922 by the union of Russian, Ukrainian, Belarusian and Transcaucasian Soviet republics, the glue that kept this gigantic country together was ideology ...and the aeroplane.

It was as early as January 17, 1921, that the Council of Peoples' Commissars, known as Sovnarkom, the highest authority in the founding years of the Soviet Union, published an important document, About Air Transportation, signed by Lenin himself. It declared sovereignty over its airspace and defined rules for the operation of foreign aircraft within its borders. It led directly to the first commercial air flights in the Soviet Union, beginning on May Day, 1921, between Moscow and Kharkov with stops in Oryol and Kursk, using Sikorsky Ilya Muromets, carrying passengers and mail. Deruluft Deutsch Russische Luftverkwehrs AG was formed in Berlin on November 11 to operate Fokker F-IIIs with both Russian and German registration, carrying mail between Konigsberg (today Kaliningrad, a Russian exclave) and Moscow via Kaunas and Smolensk twice a week, and later Berlin to Leningrad via Tallinn.

On February 3, 1923, Sovnarkom authorised the expansion of civil air operations in the Soviet Union, and this date is considered the big bang for Aeroflot, as the declaration led directly to the airline's predecessor Dobrolet on March 17, to operate passenger, airmail and cargo flying, plus agricultural and photo survey duties, with a start-up capital of two million gold rubles.

The name was a nod to the Russian Merchant Navy Volunteer Fleet, which boiled down in Russian to the shorthand Dobroflot ("Volunteer Fleet"). Famous artist and photographer Alexander Rodchenko was a member of the Enterprise for Friends of the Air Fleet steering committee and designed the iconic winged hammer and sickle logo which remains in use today by Aeroflot. Dobrolet began scheduled flying from Moscow to Nizhniy Novgorod on July 15.

A subdivision based in Tashkent in the Uzbek SSR was established the same year for services to Almaty in the neighbouring Kazakh SSR. Another, based in Sevastapol, began serving

The mammoth Tu-114 was a turboprop that served as the Soviet Union's long haul flagship from its first flight in November 1957 until the advent of the Il-62 in 1967. With generous accomodation for up to 200 passengers and near-jet speed, 32 were in service until retirement in 1976
via Don Howell

the Crimea. Other early routes included Kazan, Odessa, and Rostov-on-Don. In 1929 the airline was merged with a Ukrainian airline, Ukrpovitroshliach, and a Georgian airline, Zakavia. The biggest restructuring of the era came on October 29, 1930, when the Dobrolet brand was discarded in favour of the Chief Directorate of the Civil Air Fleet, and on March 25 1932, the last two words - Air Fleet - already in use as shorthand, were adopted as the name of the airline: Aeroflot.

While it didn't do much for mass transportation, the Tupolev ANT-20 Maxim Gorky was an eight-engine behemoth with a wingspan as wide as a Boeing 747 and first flew in May 1934. It was used for propaganda purposes, featuring its own radio station ('Voice From The Sky'), printing press, film projector and post office. Despite its gargantuan size, it could be disassembled and transported by rail. 364 days after its first flight, it crashed following a collision with a Polikarpov I-5 single-seat biplane, but in its brief lifetime gave an early indication of the ambition and creativity of the Soviet aviation establishment.

The Douglas DC-3 was licenced by the Soviet Union for local production after aeronautical engineer Boris Pavlovich Lisunov spent two years in Santa Monica translating the design.

Initially known as the PS-84, the Lisunov Li-2 was produced in Moscow (and, in World War 2 during the evacuation of Moscow, in Tashkent) beginning in 1939, with at least 5,000 built when the last machine was completed in 1952.

A homegrown replacement for the Li-2 was planned as early as the autumn of 1943 by the Ilyushin OKB, with all-metal construction, a low-wing monoplane, tricycle landing gear, and conventional tail. The result was the Il-12, which first flew on August 15, 1945, with 663 built over the next four years, in service with Aeroflot from June 1947 with seating for 21 passengers. The

East Germany's Baade 152 jetliner was built at the VEB Flugzeugwerke plant in Dresden and first flew on December 4, 1958. Three were built, and two flew, but an accident on March 4, 1959, probably due to a fault in the fuel system, cooled enthusiasm for the project, which was cancelled, despite 20 airframes in various states of completion for Interflug

type's international debut was from Moscow to Sofia the following year, and the longest flight was to Khabarovsk, a journey taking 28 hours, with five stops en route. Export sales were achieved to the flag carriers of Soviet-controlled eastern Europe, such as Malev of Hungary, LOT Polish Airlines, TAROM Romania, and TABSO in Bulgaria. 20 were sold to CAAC in China.

Despite this success, the Il-12 was underpowered and its aerofoil design lacked sophistication, and led to the Il-14, a true smash hit that saw 1,348 copies manufactured. As well as production in Moscow at Machinery Plant No. 30 and Tashkent Factory No. 84, 80 were built by VEB Flugzeugwerke in Dresden in East Germany between 1956 and 1959, and 200 by Avia Prague in Czechoslovakia between 1956 and 1960. The Il-14 remained in widespread service at least until the 1990s, and a handful remain flying today as freighters or maintained by enthusiasts.

French aerospace engineer Maxime Guillaume had patented the idea of using a turbine to power an aircraft as early as 1921, and in Britain, Alan Arnold Griffith published the ground-breaking *An Aerodynamic Theory Of Turbine Design* in 1926 for the Royal Aircraft Establishment. Fellow Brit Frank Whittle worked through the 1930s developing axial compressor designs, but the simultaneous efforts of Hans Von Ohain in Germany meant the first jet aircraft to fly was the Heinkel He-178 on August 27, 1939. The Messerschmitt Me-262 followed it into the air on July 18, 1942 and entered service as the world's first operational jet-powered fighter in April 1944. The Brits were right behind, with the Gloster Meteor entering service with the Royal Air Force (RAF) in July of the same year. The first American jet fighter was the P-59 Airacomet by Bell Aircraft Corporation of Buffalo NY, who went on to build the Bell X-1, the world's first supersonic plane.

The Soviet Union's first jet engine to be mass-produced was borrowed from Rolls-Royce. The United Kingdom was keen to improve relations with the USSR and sold sample engines, blueprints and technical data to the Kirill Klimov OKB, who quickly reverse-engineered the Rolls-Royce Nene to create the RD-45 prototype, which went into production as the VK-1 and powered the MiG-15 – 12,000 native machines and 6,000 built under licence in China, Czechoslovakia and Poland.

It didn't take long for true made-in-Russia jet technology to catch up, with the Mikulin AM-3 and AM-5 turbojets (renamed the Turmansky RD-9 after a change of leadership at the design bureau that produced it) being produced without recourse to imported technology. The Tupolev Tu-16, which first flew on April 27, 1952, was a successful bomber with 1,509 produced including export sales to Egypt, Iraq and Indonesia, plus another 180 built under licence in China as the Xian H-6 (60 years on, most H-6s are still in service with the People's Liberation Army Air Force). With the Tu-16 and its powerplant rapidly becoming established technology, the Soviet Union's jet-powered civil airliner ambitions were off to the races.

Aeroflot postcard — Noel Marsh-Giddings

Aeroflot's introduction of the Tupolev Tu-104 on September 15 1956 under the command of Boris Bugayev, Leonid Brezhnev's personal pilot, on the long route from Moscow to Irkutsk via Omsk, put the Soviet Union ahead of every other nation in the world, until Britain reintroduced the de Havilland Comet to revenue service on October 4 1958, and the United States entered the Jet Age a few weeks after that with the Boeing 707 on October 26.

In the Soviet Union, growth was driven by enormous demand. By the end of 1958, Aeroflot had a network covering 349,000 kilometres (217,000 miles) and carried 8,231,500 passengers, and 445,600 tons of mail and freight. 15% of the airline's capacity was jet powered. In a big country, jets made a difference that is hard to exaggerate. In the propeller age, Yekaterinburg was the furthest city from Moscow to be served nonstop, 1770 kilometres to the east. With the advent of the Tu-104, a letter posted in Moscow could reach Vladivostok, on the Pacific Ocean, on the same day.

By 1961, passenger numbers hit 21,800,000, and in 1964, 36,800,000, with direct flights from Moscow to 100 cities, from Leningrad to 44, and from Kiev 38. Unlike in the West, most of the traffic wasn't travellers paying out of their own pocket to fly. International travel was extremely problematic for the average Soviet citizen, and domestic flying was expensive, with a typical fare costing as much as two weeks' typical salary. Nonetheless, travel by air was accessible to many through political or occupational affiliation, for study, work, prison, or leisure (by 1964, spa town Mineralnye Vody, gateway to the Caucasian Mineral Waters, had nonstop service to 48 cities).

In the high summer season of 1970, Aeroflot was flying 400,000 people a day, and 100 million for the year, and traffic kept growing. Those numbers may seem exaggerated but bear in mind that including props, the Aeroflot fleet numbered into the thousands.

Not only was the entire Soviet Union stitched together and even if most of the traffic overall was domestic, much of the rest of the world was linked to Moscow and the rest of the Soviet Union by air – the glamourous capitals of western Europe, the sprawling megalopolises of the Indian subcontinent and southeast Asia, Tokyo, Montreal, Havana, Mexico City.

Baku Airport in 1976; the Tu-154, CCCP-85169, was lost on a flight to Leningrad on May 19 1978 when the tanks ran dry and the aircraft glided to a crash landing (four killed) **Valentin Grebnev** Transport-Photo Images

■ Classic Aeroflot line up in the year of the 1980 Moscow Olympics **Valentin Grebnev** Transport-Photo Images

■ Four crew at work aboard Il-86 RA-86125 **Fyodor Borisov** Transport-Photo Images

A busy ramp at Kiev Borispol in the 1980s
B. Korzin Transport-Photo Images

Balkan Bulgarian ramp scene
Mark J Nutter

SXF in snow

A unique feature of the route map: Aeroflot's famous fortnightly Tu-154 flights to the furthest reaches of Soviet influence in sub-Saharan Africa. Not enough traffic for a weekly flight? No problem!

The hardware produced by the Soviet Union wasn't the exclusive preserve of Aeroflot. Picture an Interflug Il-62 leaving Hanoi in the morning and chasing the sun all day across Eurasia, with a short leg to Dhaka in Bangladesh followed by a midday stop and crew change in Karachi, then a long afternoon cruise to Berlin Schönefeld, blocking in after dark, the handful of passengers (and a couple of Stasi sky marshalls in plain clothes, albeit easy to spot) wearily clambering down the steps to the damp German tarmac, and, after tiresome immigration formalities, swallowed up by the small line of Trabant taxis waiting outside arrivals to take them to the Berlin Stadt Interhotel, to a military base, to apartments in the marching tower blocks of East Berlin. Not to forget the West Germans taking advantage of Interflug's cheap

A 1978 advert for CSA showing an Il-62 on the ramp in Havana   **Guy Van Herbruggen Collection**

Night turnaround at Sheremetyevo in the 1990s   **Pavel Novikov** Transport-Photo Images

fares, who would be channeled directly onto a late Interflug bus that would take them through Checkpoint Charlie to their homes in West Berlin on the other side of the Wall.

Interflug's sole transatlantic route was to Havana via Gander, a small frozen Canadian town in Newfoundland on the Atlantic coast, whose sole purpose seemed to be providing fuel for jetliners. A few East Germans used the stopover to defect to the West. In a horrible but somehow comedic twist, it's believed that once or twice, a family pragmatically enjoyed their holiday in sunny Cuba before defecting on the return journey; imagine the horror of boarding the flight in Havana, ready to prostrate themselves before a Canadian immigration offical, only to hear the captain cheerfully announce, due to strong tailwinds this evening our flight back to Berlin will operate nonstop (and we will arrive ahead of schedule!).

The German Democratic Republic wasn't the only socialist airline flying long haul – Czechoslovakia's CSA smoked their way east all the way to Jakarta with Il-18s, later Tu-124s, and finally Il-62s, and Choson Minhang (CAAK) of North Korea did the same in reverse with their Il-18s (which are still performing local service in 2018) from Pyongyang to Berlin via Moscow. LOT were flying Il-62s to New York and Toronto as early as 1973, and Cubana served South America, Tenerife (where a sizeable Cuban community resides) and Madrid with their Il-62s. (Having moved into the Soviet sphere later than the rest, Cubana's original longhaul equipment was the Bristol Britannia!)

In hindsight, the division of Europe was never going to stick, even if the balance of power achieved a remarkably locked-in symmetry for many decades. Uprisings in East Berlin as early as 1953, Hungary in 1956 and the Prague Spring of 1968 may not have seemed like it at the time but were actually signs of things to come. The end of the post-World War 2 impasse began in earnest with dockworkers' strikes in Poland in 1980. The widening shortfall in material quality of life compared to the West, and a frustration with the lack of freedom of speech and freedom of movement, drove a wave of disobedience and eventually, open protest, especially in East Germany, where comparison with the wealth and opportunity experienced by West Germans was more unflattering with each passing year. The Berlin Wall and Inner German Border were the most tangible symbols of the Cold War and the division of Europe; so when an East German spokesperson accidentally announced the opening of the Berlin Wall on the evening of November 9, 1989, the floodgates couldn't be closed and German

SibNIA's Yak-42 RA-42440 inflight at 26,000 feet on a research flight on behalf of the Federal Service for Hydrometeorology and Environmental Monitoring of Russia
Yevgeny Lebedev

reunification heralded the start of a new age.

By early 1990, Soviet republics followed suit and began declaring independence from the mothership, starting with Lithuania, followed by Baltic neighbours Estonia and Latvia in March, then Armenia. In 1991 the rest fell like dominos, with Belarus, Ukraine, Moldova, Kyrgyzstan in a few days in August, followed by Uzbekistan, Azerbaijan, Tajikistan in September and Turkmenistan in October. On December 8, the leaders of Russia, Ukraine and Belarus met in Belarus to sign the Belavezha Accords which declared the Soviet Union to no longer exist, replaced by a so-called Commonwealth Of Independent States (CIS), which was reinforced by the Alma-Ata Protocol, signed by 11 of the 12 Soviet republics (omitting Georgia) on December 21. In the early hours of Christmas Day, Mikhail S. Gorbachev resigned as president of the Soviet Union in a nationally televised speech, ceding power to Boris N. Yeltsin who had been elected president of Russia in June. After Gorbachev left the Kremlin government headquarters in Moscow that evening, the Soviet flag was lowered from the flagpole for the last time and the Russian tricolour was raised in its place. The Soviet Union was over.

The years that followed – the 1990s – were suitably turbulent in the wake of such a momentous change, as the founding ideology of a socialist mega-state driven by the elite of a one-party system turned to rampant free market capitalism.

Aeroflot, at the time the Soviet Union broke up, had a fleet of 2,500 jet airliners, 2,500 turboprops, and 9,000 helicopters and smaller fixed-wing craft (agricultural, survey, training), with 500,000 employees – comparable in scale to the entire airline scene in western Europe or the United States. (In the same year – 1990 – Pan Am had 152 planes.)

The airline network of Russia and the newly independent sovereign states on its borders, the break-up of Aeroflot and deregulation gave rise to literally hundreds of small carriers. At the high end, locally-based Aeroflot planes were appropriated by local governments to

Ramp line up at Krasnoyarsk airport starring the hometown team

Leonid Faerberg Transport-Photo Images

create new national airlines, such as Armavia, Uzbekistan Airways and Air Ukraine, or within Russia by local authorities or businessmen to form independent airlines such as Bashkirian Airlines, Omskavia, Arkhangelsk Airlines, Petropavlovsk-Kamchatsky Air Enterprise to name but a tiny handful. Some sustained and went on to greatness, such as Siberian Airlines which became S7, today a globally-known brand to rival Aeroflot and member of the oneworld alliance. At the other end of the spectrum were tiny one- or two-ship fleets in provincial parts of the still-enormous Russia, a high time Tu-134 reactivated by a local factory to create a travel club charter operation, a line-up of Yak-40s surplus from a mining enterprise becoming an air taxi and regional commuter set up, or a provincial government flagging a handful of Yak-42s or Tu-154s to enhance economic and cultural links to the rest of Russia.

Another example of the region's improvised 1990s airline scene were outfits who were able to inherit Soviet-built machines when their local national carrier bought their first Boeing and Airbus. The airline industry in the Czech Republic experienced one such glut of capacity when flag carrier CSA unloaded their obsolescent Il-62s onto start-ups such as Georgia Air Prague, Espo Air, Ensor Air, IDG Technology Airlines and Egretta BMI Bemoair, none of whom could probably believe their luck at finding themselves owner-operators of a four-engined jetliner that could fly halfway round the world, and acquired for next to nothing. These were flown on charter flights to sunshine destinations in the Mediterranean or on sports charters to elsewhere in Europe for a game, a degree of mobility unthinkable just a couple of years earlier.

These upstarts held on for a few years before the cost of fuel and maintenance – reality – intervened. These elderly and very thirsty jetliners were optimised to operate as a part of a monolithic national airline such as Aeroflot with unlimited manpower and spare parts, not a glorified flying club. One by one they parked their once-proud

A look at the future of Russian aviation as a Sukhoi SSJ flies in formation with a Tu-204 at Zhukovsky
Fyodor Borisov Transport-Photo Images

birds for storage or scrapping.

While the Soviet system failed its citizens in providing a high standard of living or much in the way of personal freedom, its scientific achievements should not be overlooked, and in few arenas were they as outstanding as in flight. In spaceflight it was a clean sweep: Sputnik followed by the first animal, man, woman, and multi-person crew in space. The first spaceship formation flight, the first space station, first probe to hit another planet (Venus), first probe to make a soft landing and transmit from the Moon. Even as the USSR was stagnating in the 1980s, it was still pioneering, with the first crew to visit two different space stations (*Mir* and *Salyut 7*), the first crew to spend over a year in space, the first permanently manned space station.

Today Soviet jetliners are remembered with great nostalgia as the current civil aviation scene sees conventional wisdom converge, and every airliner looks the same. A layperson might be able to look at an unmarked A350 and a 787 yet somehow sense that they are surveying two different machines, but would struggle to point out the actual differences. A more blended wing-to-body join here, a serated cowling edge there. On the other hand, the airliners detailed in this book are completely different to each other, and all are striking, aggressive, confident. More importantly, they were all safe, capable, and, by the expectations of the time, efficient.

Today's airline scene uses hardware which is incredible in its productivity and safety (not a single fatality on a commercial jet in 2017 anywhere in the world), but for the human senses, something has been lost. In terms of safety and efficiency, the Soviet fleet were comparable to their Western counterparts, so one can accept those as a given; but for noise smoke and great looks, the classic Tupolevs, Ilyushins and Yakovlevs – the jetliners of the red star – will never be beaten.

Charles Kennedy, June 2019
Baker St London & Claygate Surrey, England

A Tu-204 lands at sunset
Artyom Kuzhlev

Valentin Grebnev Transport-Photo Images

Tupolev Tu-104 & -124
The start of the art

The Soviet Union had early experience of jet-powered bombers, including the Myasischev M-4 and Tupolev Tu-16, but the 1950s civilian air fleet serving the biggest country the world has ever seen – spanning eleven time zones – comprised small and slow piston-driven Lisunov Li-2s, Ilyushin Il-12s and -14s.

Aerospace design legend Andrei N. Tupolev approached the Communist Party Central Committee in early 1953 to propose a jet airliner initially known as "aircraft 104" based on the Tu-16, with much of the technology transferrable to the civilian project. The two decisive advantages of a jet airliner were the ability to fly twice as fast as any propliner, and twice as high. An additional factor was the longer service life of jets due to the relative simplicity of the powerplant.

On June 11, 1954, the Soviet Council Of Ministers released directive no. 1172-516 for construction of an airliner based on the Tu-16, known as the Tu-16P, using Mikulin AM-3-200 turbojet engines. The new jetliner would be built at factory number 135 "Lenin Komsomol" in Kharkov. Major components were supplied by Tu-16 plants: Factory No. 1 in Kuibyshev (today Aviacor in Samara) and the famous Factory No. 22 in Kazan. This was probably the last aircraft to be approved by Joseph Stalin, who ruled the Soviet Union from 1922 until his death in March 1953.

An early mock-up used a Tu-4 (a reverse-engineered piston-powered copy of the Boeing B-29 bomber) fuselage mated to the wings and tail of a Tu-16; the hybrid was met with derision and a more sophisticated mock-up in December 1954 received a more positive response from the higher ups in the Soviet hierarchy. Soon after, the aircraft was designated the Tu-104, and NATO assigned a reporting name: Camel.

The final layout used a new fuselage with a diameter of 3.5 metres (11 feet, 5.75 inches) and a low wing with a 37 degree sweep that included an engine buried in a nacelle in each wing root. The Tu-104 was the first Tupolev to use the distinctive main landing gear design which saw the gear retract by rotating rearward through 180 degrees to lie in a pointed fairing projecting beyond the wing trailing edge.

After the Comet 1 inflight breakups, metal fatigue was a concern. The Soviet aircraft industry realised their own lack of experience in this field was a danger, so a programme to closely monitor the early-build machines was devised. Indeed the field of metal fatigue was pretty much unknown territory for everyone, with the exception of the British who at the time were in the midst of a very grisly education on the subject. Later, when the cause of the Comet disasters was fully understood, the British shared their findings with the whole world, regardless of the divisions of the Cold

War. Setting aside both political and commercial concerns helped the entire world's aviation industry evolve.

It was assumed that the area of the aircraft with the biggest risk of suffering an inflight decompression due to a failed window or door was the cockpit and navigator's station in the nose with its expanse of glass, so the divider at the rear of the cockpit was a pressure bulkhead, thereby reducing or totally halting the loss of pressure in the passenger cabin in the event of an explosive decompression; as a result, the cockpit door was as heavy as a bank safe.

Although early aircraft were fitted with passenger oxygen, Minister Of Aviation Yeveiny Loginov decreed it was unnecessary and a fire hazard, and the safety provision was taken out of production.

Given how ahead of its time and capable it was, only omissions or differences such as the lack of passenger oxygen masks stopped the Tu-104 from being a bigger export success – a Western Europe / North America-compliant Tu-104 could have been a big seller. (To be fair, early British and French jetliners including most BAC One Elevens and some Caravelles did not have passenger oxygen masks until US sales came calling, American Airlines for One-Elevens and United Airlines for Caravelles, and such safety equipment became standard. Also Concorde was never fitted with personal oxygen masks for passengers.)

Prototype CCCP-L5400 was built at Moscow Machinery Plant MMZ No. 156 at the beginning of 1955. After checks, engine runs and taxiing under its own power, the machine was dismantled and trucked to the airfield at Zhukovsky for flight testing at the Mikhail M. Gromov Flight Research Institute.

On June 17, 1955, The Tupolev Tu-104 became the sixth jetliner to take flight, following the Vickers Type 618 Nene-Viking, the de Havilland Comet 1, the Avro Canada C-102 Jetliner, the Boeing 367-80 and the Sud Aviation Caravelle. Under the command of Captain Yuriy T Alasheyev and joined by first officer Boris M. Timoshok, navigator P N Roodnev, flight engineer I R Ivanov, radio operator V P Yevgafov, and test engineers V N Benderov and B F Petrov, the 37 minute flight was a complete success. The public debut for the Soviet Union's new people's jetliner followed on July 3 at the Aviation Day flypast at Moscow-Tushino.

Up to October 12, 1955, 74 hours and 55 minutes were logged on 41 flights. Some minor bumps along the way included loss of all speed data on a few early flights, and troubles with the avionics such as comms or navigation radios failing. Events such as these were expected and easily rectified, and some improvements to the effectiveness of the controls were made.

The prototype was submitted to the Air Force State Research Institute at Chkalovskaya east of Moscow on January 31, 1956 for evaluation. These trials were captained by Major A. K. Starikov, who had also overseen the certification of the Tu-16 jet bomber. More than 100 flights totalling 180 hours saw the evaluation of single engine flight, fuel dumping, emergency descent, high speed

■ A Tu-104 flyover on July 9, 1961 during the Moscow air parade at Tushino   **Lev Polikashin RIAN Archive**

■ Tu-104A CCCP-42463 flew for Aeroflot from May 23 1960 until retirement in 1979, seen in Stockholm, July 1966   **Lars Soderstrom**

rejected takeoffs, stalls, flying in icing conditions, and airframe structural strength (in addition, two years of water tank tests on a static airframe at TsAGI simulated 7,200 flight cycles).

The Tu-104's first international trip took place on March 22 with a flight to London Heathrow, carrying a delegation led by the head of the KGB, General Ivan Serov, flying into London to make security arrangements for the forthcoming state visit to Britain by Soviet premier Nikita Khrushchev. The development thus far of the Tu-104 had mostly been done out of sight of the western world, and most observers were genuinely amazed by the machine that turned up at Heathrow that day. British newspapers breathlessly reported on "Russia's Secret Plane!"

The commander of the London mission was Captain A. K. Stariov who was in charge of

■ Tu-104B turnaround on the ramp at Simferopol; this bird entered the Aeroflot fleet on on March 24 1960 and served right up to the type's retirement in 1980   **Valentin Grebnev** Transport-Photo Images

training flight crews and overseeing the training of other technical roles for the introduction of the new jet. Some training was accomplished using a civilianised Tupolev Tu-16 bomber, known as the Tu-104G (G for Grazhdanskiy, "civil"), and more commonly by those who flew it as the Little Red Riding Hood (a reference to the fairy tale in which a wolf disguises itself as a grandmother).

The certification process ended with the Tu-104 cleared for passenger flight on June 15, 1956. The first revenue flight was operated on September 15, operating in place of a piston-driven Ilyushin Il-14, from Moscow to Irkutsk via Omsk, a total journey of 2,667 miles (4,292 km). The new jetliner reduced the trip time from 13 hours and 50 minutes to just seven hours and 40 minutes, an excellent example of the essential role the jet engine played in bringing the far-flung parts of Russia and its empire together.

The early Tu-104 passenger cabin was divided into two small compartments ahead of the wing with six and eight seats with tables, followed by an eight seat cabin aft of the wing, followed by a main cabin which seated 28 in paired seats either side of the aisle. The interior design was dubbed "Homestyle", and was also known as "Imperial Style" and featured gilded decor, walnut panels, leaded glass, heavy brass embellishments, lace seat covers and Plexiglass display cabinets containing various ornaments. The result resembled a Victorian rail carriage. God knows what such luxury added to the weight of the aircraft.

The impact of the Tu-104 on every aspect of Soviet life cannot be exaggerated. The sixth Five Year Plan (1956-1960) called for an expansion of Aeroflot's role in all spheres of economic activity. Modernisation of airport and en route facilities were implemented across the country, starting with 80 airfields identified as most in need of upgrade. Some of this infrastructure is still in use to this day.

By the end of 1956, Aeroflot was flying over 20 airframes on an ever-expanding network of routes with the Soviet Union, and a growing number of international flights, starting with Prague on October 12.

The Tupolev OKB went to work on an upgraded Tu-104A, which retained the same fuselage as the baseline model but with an updated interior influenced by western cabin architecture, and also by the perception of luxury being considered "undemocratic", and "bourgeois" in the communist state. This paved the way for a more austere, functional, and high density passenger

■ CCCP-42395 flew for Aeroflot for two decades right up to the retirement of the type in 1979   Brussels **Guy Viselé**

interior which could seat 70 passengers. The Mikulin AM-3 powerplants were replaced by the uprated AM-3M. The first revenue flight of a Tu-104A was by CCCP-L5421 out of Moscow-Vnukovo on July 10, 1957.

A Tu-104A made the first Atlantic crossing by a Soviet civil transport since the start of World War Two when CCCP-L5438 flew a delegation to the United Nations in New York, causing a similar commotion on its arrival at Wrightstown McGuire AFB on September 4, 1957 as the original prototype had at Heathrow the previous year. (Ten days later another Tu-104 made the same trip, this time bringing in the Soviet Foreign Minister.)

After fanning out across the domestic Aeroflot network, the first Tu-104A international destination was the Albanian capital of Tirana, followed by a stopping service across the Soviet Union that terminated in the Chinese capital of Beijing. Cairo and Delhi were also early destinations for the Tu-104A.

The only export customer for the Tu-104 was the Czechoslovakian airline CSA, something of a 'star pupil' among airlines in the communist world, who took three Tu-104As starting with OK-LDA, delivered to Prague on November 2, 1957. CSA's first jet flight was operated on December 9 to Moscow. Ultimately the Czechoslovakian flag carrier operated six of the type – four new and two second-hand. Their last three were retired in April 1974.

■ Tu-104 brochure

A N. Tupolev put one of his top men, Dmitri Markov (later chief engineer on the Tu-154 programme) in charge of developing a radical new variant, a four-engine machine with extended range, for intercontinental trips and with an eye on serious export sales, designated the Tu-110,

■ Tu-110

■ Vnukovo Airport seen, June 1 1971   **Lev Polikashin**

NATO reporting name Cookpot, authorised for production at the Kazan aircraft factory by the Council of Ministers with directive 1511-846, issued on August 12, 1956.

The powerplant selected for the four-engined variant was the Lyulska AL-5, rated at 10,150 lbs (4,600 kgs) of thrust each, and the fuselage was stretched by 1.2 metres (3.9 feet) to increase passenger capacity. The wing was enhanced with a widened chord and a greater flap area, with some window rearrangements and internal changes which allowed five abreast seating instead of four, bringing passenger capacity up to 100 – 30 in the forward cabin, 15 over the wing, and 55 in the rear cabin.

Despite these enhancements, after the massive investment in ground and en route infrastructure needed to assure safe and reliable operations for the Tu-104, there was no appetite for another new type so soon, despite swapping out the Lyulska engines in favour of more powerful Soloviev D-20s. By the time the first Tu-110 took to the air for the first time on March 11, 1957, it was understood that the type would not enter passenger service, so it was given the military registration of 5600 and a red star for the tail. After the completion of trials, this aircraft was delivered to the Kiev Institute of Civil Aviation Engineering where it was used as a flying testbed for experimental work on avionics, missile systems, boundary layer control systems, and other projects.

All was not lost, however, as the fuselage stretch and new wing developed for the Tu-110 were incorporated into the Tu-104B. The uprated AM-3M-500 turbojet meant field performance stayed the same as on the lighter Tu-104A despite the extra structural weight and payload.

The Tu-104B was not widely seen on international sectors; rather, with its high passenger capacity, it was used a domestic people mover on trunk routes within the Soviet Union, starting with the busiest route in the network, Moscow to Leningrad (today Saint Petersburg) on April 15, 1959.

Despite the failure of the Tu-110 to reach production, the ever-ambitious Tupolev OKB saw another niche in jet-powered air transport, and this time their efforts to create a new variant of the Tu-104 bore fruit. The Tu-104 was doing a fine job flying on mainline routes but smaller, thinner city pairs were still without jet service, and on July 18, 1958, the Soviet Council of Ministers issued Directive No. 786-378 for the creation of a smaller, lighter jetliner to fill that gap, to be known as the Tu-124.

Tu-110 sales brochure from the 1958 Brussels Expo

via Bruno Vandermueren

■ OK-LDA was CSA's first Tu-104A and served the Czechoslovakian airline from delivery on November 2, 1957, until retirement on September 14, 1973, and is preserved at the Letecke Museum in Kbely, seen in Stockholm, November 1970 **Lars Soderstrom**

■ V644 was one of three Tu-124s operated by the Indian Air Force and today is preserved at Palam **Richard Vandervord**

■ CSA's Tu-124V OK-UEC was delivered in 1965 and sold to Aeroflot in 1973 **Guy Viselé**

The aim was to create an 80% sized 'scale model' of the Tu-104 but only weighing half as much. The Soloviev D-20 turbofan was selected as the powerplant, making the Tu-124 the world's first turbofan-powered airliner. The prototype was built at the Moscow Machinery Plant MMZ No. 156 even as the first production models began to take shape on the line at Kharkov. Prototype CCCP-45000 was trucked to the Gromov Flight Research Institute at Zhukovsky and flew for the first time on March 29, 1960 under the command of test pilot A. D. Markov. Four production models joined the test programme (two of which were used as static test frames) which was followed by state test trials which ended in September 1962.

The first revenue service for the Tu-124 took place on October 2 on the route from Moscow to Tallinn, marking the beginning of a successful career with Aeroflot, filling two separate niches – flying on prestigious international flights to the likes of Warsaw, East Berlin and Prague, and also bringing jet service to many smaller cities throughout the Soviet Union for the first time.

Despite a low purchase price, the Tu-124 was not a big export success, selling only to CSA in Czechoslovakia and Interflug in East Germany. Interflug sold their pair back to Aeroflot, and CSA sold their three to Iraqi Airways who used them as a VIP fleet until 1990. Three other VIP machines were sold to the Indian Air Force for use up until 1980, and the Chinese Air Force took two for use as navigational trainers, retired in 1990.

In the spring of 1961, Aeroflot began a heavy modification programme to modernise the Tu-104A fleet. Under the direction of aerospace engineer Kh. Izmiryan, the fleet was gradually reworked to accommodate 100 passengers in a similar configuration to the Tu-104B; this upgrade was redesigned as the Tu-104V. A further upgrade to these same machines began in late 1964 when they were retrofitted with the uprated AM-3M-500 engines and fitted with 85 passenger seats; these machines were known as Tu-104Ds. They were first delivered to the Ukrainian Directorate of Aeroflot and introduced on routes out of Odessa, initially to Moscow and shortly followed by Leningrad.

A Tu-124Sh cockpit   Andrew Babin

In 1966, Aeroflot's chief engineer at their Vnukovo base, A. K. Musatov, was tasked with reworking the Tu-104B fleet to carry 104 passengers, and in March 1967 it was announced that some Tu-104Bs could now carry 115, close to double the accommodation provided on early Tu-104s.

The Tu-104 family proved to be very reliable in airline service. Time between engine overhaul was initially set at a conservative 300 hours, and extended in stages to 2,000 hours. In 1964, the first Tu-104 that had been delivered to Aeroflot (originally CCCP-L5412, later reregistered CCCP-42318) was withdrawn from service to be part of a research programme to check the airframe's design life. It was placed in a water tank and pressurised and depressurised to simulate the effects of flight cycles. Although the Tu-104 was designed before the Comet 1 suffered its disastrous series of crashes caused by metal fatigue, no structural weaknesses were found.

Being at the forefront of new technology was not without a price – the aerodynamic properties of the Soviet Union's first jetliner could bite. On May 16, 1958, both engines on a CSA Tu-104A flamed out in turbulence; one engine was relit and an emergency landing was made at a Czechoslovakian air force base. On June 22 another Tu-104A, this time in Aeroflot service, stalled after hitting a powerful updraft in the cruise at 12,500 metres (41,010 feet) and lost 2,000 metres (6,561 feet) before recovering.

■ DM-SDA, seen here in Prague, carried Interflug livery as a disguise but flew for the East German government and air force, then with Aeroflot from 1975 until retirement in September 1983
Jacques Barbé

■ CCCP-45070 was a Tu-124V that served Aeroflot's international network from December 12, 1964, until 1977, seen here at the end of winter, Stockholm April 1966
Lars Soderstrom

Luck ran out on August 15 when CCCP-42349 stalled after encountering turbulent air and fell 12,000 metres (39,370 feet) in a flat spin to crash near the southern Siberian city of Chita. On October 17, a similar fate befell CCCP-42362 near Kazan. Although airliners of the era did not have black box flight data recorders, the radio operator on the second flight broadcast the situation and pilot actions throughout the emergency – the calls were taped by the control tower and the radio operator's brave actions helped the investigation immeasurably.

A service ceiling restriction of 10,000 metres (32,808 feet) was put in place, the aft centre of gravity position was limited to 25.6% instead of 30%, maximum stabiliser incidence was reduced from two degrees to one degree, and to assist in unusual attitude recovery, elevator travel limits were increased by three degrees. Also, the old-style AGB attitude indicators (also known as the artificial horizon) inherited from bombers were replaced by AGI-1 fighter-type instruments.

These modifications and limitations were based partly on the valuable data gained from a series of test flights with the prototype CCCP-L5400 flown by Y. T. Alasheyev and V. F. Kovalyov, overseen by test engineer V. N. Vendorov, and CCCP-L5421 which was flown by S. N. Anokhin, V. A. Komarov and V. F. Khapov, overseen by test engineer Yu. G. Yefimov. In one test flight, CCCP-L5421 stalled and flipped completely inverted; skipper Kovalyov was able to recover the aircraft and land safely. The machine staying intact throughout such an extreme series of manoeuvres is testament to the strength of the Tu-104.

Other shortcomings revealed by entry into service, such as the tendency of the landing gear to deploy when subjected to high G loads, and the lack of a flap sequencing system to prevent asymmetrical flap extension, were addressed during the evolution of the type.

Despite these improvements, the pioneering nature of the age meant there were plenty of other ways airliners could be lost in service, and accidents for various other reasons continued to occur, much as they did to early jets in the West such as the 707 and DC-8. On March 16, 1961, an engine explosion on CCCP-42438 led to an emergency landing on a frozen lake which ended in disaster; on October 3, 1962, CCCP-42366 crashed near Khabarovsk with the loss of all aboard, probably due to problems with the autopilot, but could have accidentally been shot down, a fate which was positively identified as the reason for

■ TU-104B CCCP-42416 in a support role at the 1975 Paris Air Show in the final livery to be worn by the type   **Jacques Barbé**

This Tu-104 was built in 1956 and is preserved at Kiev Zhuliany CCCP-L5415   Guy Viselé

the loss of CCCP-42370 three months earlier over Krasnoyarsk. On October 25, 1962, CCCP-42495 crashed immediately after takeoff from Moscow Sheremetyevo due to the aileron control rods being fitted incorrectly.

Up until 1973, each aircraft type in the Aeroflot fleet had a different livery, but in that year, the classic navy cheatline was adopted fleet-wide and most late-build Tu-104s stayed in service long enough to be repainted in that scheme.

The Tu-104 was withdrawn from airline service after a fatal crash in Moscow on March 17, 1979 that was initiated by a false fire alarm in one engine and ended with a poorly flown emergency approach and landing that resulted in a crash that killed 58 of the 113 souls onboard. Since the last Tu-104s were ready to be stood down anyway, the accident only hastened the retirement date by months.

Plenty of airframes had migrated to the Soviet Air Force, Soviet Navy, and various industrial and party organisations and so the type flew on in Soviet skies for a few more years. However this was brought to an end by another accident which took place on February 17, 1981, when Tu-104D CCCP-42332 was operating a flight on behalf of the Soviet Navy and crashed at Pushkin, near Leningrad, due to asymmetrical flap retraction which caused the aircraft to roll immediately after getting airborne; at low speed, there was not enough aileron authority available to counter the bank and the aircraft crashed with the loss of all 51 onboard. All Tu-104 flying in the Soviet Union came to an end.

The last flight of a Tu-104 was performed by CCCP-42322, a Tu-104A, which had been parked at an airfield near Murmansk, and was returned to flight condition to be ferried via Moscow SVO to the Civil Air Fleet Museum at Ulyanovsk on November 11, 1986, with Tu-134A CCCP-65047 belonging to the State Scientific Test Institute for the Civil Air Fleet (known in Russian shorthand as the GosNII) flying alongside as a chase plane. Iraqi, Indian and Chinese military Tu-124s remained in service for a few more years but were all parked by 1990, bringing an end to 35 years of service for the pioneering Soviet jet.

The Tu-104 was the glue in the Soviet Union, bringing cities together in a matter of hours that previously took days to travel between. By the time of its retirement in 1980, the type had performed 600,000 flights, spent two million hours in the air, and carried 100 million passengers and countless thousands of tonnes of cargo. It was an undoubted commercial success too, with 201 Tu-104s produced, plus 164 Tu-124s and four Tu-110s for a total of 369 airframes, an impressive number, especially for the era. The Tu-104 deserves a place in aviation history for being the world's first jet airliner to provide safe and sustained public transport.

Alexander Mishin

Tupolev Tu-134
The fighter jet

The Tupolev Tu-134 traces its origins to the state visit of Soviet premier Nikita Khrushchev to France in January 1960. The Soviet Union had made aviation history with the Tu-104 which was the world's first jetliner to provide sustained and successful service, and again with the first turbofan-powered jetliner with its smaller and lighter sister, the Tu-124. But Khrushchev was impressed by Sud Aviation's Caravelle twinjet, which benefited from having its pair of Rolls-Royce Avon engines mounted on either side at the rear of the fuselage, making the passenger cabin almost completely silent, whereas the Tu-104V that flew him to and from France had its engines installed in the wing root alongside the passenger accommodation, making for a rather noisy ride.

Upon his return to Moscow, Khrushchev met with Andrei Tupolev and asked him to start work on a new jetliner that would approximately match the configuration of the Caravelle. The Soviet Council of Ministers formally issued Directive No. 846-341 instructing the Tupolev OKB to start work on a new short haul jet airliner with a top speed of 1,000 kmh (620 mph) and a cruise speed of 900 kmh (560 mph), a service ceiling of 12,000 metres (39,370 feet), a range of 1,500 km (930 miles) with 30 minutes of reserve fuel, and to be able to operate out of runways as short as 800 metres (2,625 feet).

Because the fuselage was taken wholesale from the then-yet to fly Tu-124, the new design was initially designated Tu-124A. (Because the Tu-124 and the Tu-134 had the same 2.9 metre (9 feet 6 inches) diameter fuselage as the Tu-4 bomber, a reverse-engineered Boeing B-29 bomber, one could say the Tu-124 and -134 are distant relatives of Boeing too.)

The engines selected for the new design were the Soloviev D-20s used on the Tu-124, but instead mounted on the rear fuselage, which meant the horizontal stabiliser had to be moved up to the top of the vertical tail (the Caravelle's cruciform placement halfway up the tail was discarded as it was thought positioning the horizontal stabiliser so close to the engines could cause fatigue due to proximity of the sound waves).

Not having the engines impinging on the wing design increased the area of the wing available for high lift devices such as trailing edge flaps, and enabled a general wing redesign incorporating the latest aerodynamic breakthroughs. Additional perceived advantages of the new engine placement included improved engine operating conditions due to the shorter inlet ducts, reduced foreign object damage (widely known as FOD) and easier access for maintenance and engine changes. Although the Tu-104 and -124 never suffered a disastrous uncontained engine failure, there was no longer any danger of fragments entering the cabin in such an event. Most of all, passenger comfort was greatly enhanced by low noise and vibration.

There were some attendant disadvantages with the new configuration too, such as an awkwardly rearward centre of gravity with so much structural weight positioned so far aft. The high position of the thrust line produced a pitch-down force that resulted in a higher takeoff speed and required beefed-up elevator control authority.

During 1961 and 1962 the size and capacity of the type, still designated the Tu-124A, crept upwards. In December 1962 the project, thus far supervised by Dmitry S. Markov, was taken over by Leonid L. Selyakov for whom this aircraft became his life's work, overseeing the development and service life of the Tu-134 through the decades ahead.

The first prototype was designated CCCP-45075 and assembled in the first half of 1963. Although only a few short years into the jet age, technology had evolved sufficiently that it was apparent that this was a new type, not just a variation, and on February 20 was redesignated the Tu-134.

Thus renamed, the Tupolev OKB's latest offspring left the nest and took to the air for the first time on July 29 under the command of Merited Test Pilot Aleksandr D Kalina.

Data from the manufacturer's trial period (which ended on November 6, 1964) was used to incorporate changes to the design into the second prototype, CCCP-45076, which was built at Factory No. 135 in Khakov and first flew from its Sokolnikovo airfield on September 9, 1964. One requirement identified was the need for more thrust, and untried D-20P-125 series 5 engines were used on the second machine.

The Tu-134 was unveiled to the world in France where its inspiration began — at the 25th Paris Airshow at Le Bourget. CCCP-45076 flew in on May 4, 1965 to a generally positive reaction from the international aviation community, then continued on to Berlin, Warsaw and Prague to visit future export customers Interflug, LOT and CSA at their home bases.

Tragedy struck the programme on January 14, 1966, when CCCP-45076 crashed 20 miles northeast of Moscow while under the review of an air force test flight authority. The handling pilot deflected the rudder a full 25 degrees to the left

This rare TU-134A CCCP-65667 was shown in full Aeroflot livery at the Paris Air Show in June 1973 but remained as an test airframe and transport for the use of the Tupolev design bureau until it was scrapped in 1999   **Jacques Barbé**

■ Early-build Tu-134 sans-suffix CCCP-65627 was delivered to Aeroflot in June 1969 and is seen here in Brussels in August 1973
Jacques Barbé

■ Busy Tu-134 action on the ramp at Kishinev Airport   **Valentin Grebnev** Transport-Photo Images

This Tu-134, registered SP-LGB, was delivered to LOT in 1968 and crashed on landing in Warsaw on January 23, 1980, luckily without any loss of life. Here she is seen taxiing at Paris Le Bourget on October 17, 1970   **Jacques Barbé**

at high speed which caused the aircraft to depart from controlled flight, entering a sharp descending turn which was not recoverable. All eight onboard were killed. The accident was not the result of a flaw with the aircraft, which may have come as a relief to the designers but added to the tragedy as there was little to be learned.

The first pre-production machine, CCCP-65600, made its first flight from Sokolnikovo on August 14, 1965, followed by CCCP-65601 shortly after. The third pre-production machine, CCCP-65603, incorporated the jet engine that would go on to power most of the Soviet Union's jetliners, the Soloviev D-30, and this pioneer lifted into Ukrainian skies over Kharkov on July 21, 1966.

British Aircraft Corporation's BAC-111 prototype G-ASHG had suffered a crash during its test flying programme on October 22, 1963 when

LZ-TUA was Balkan's first Tu-134, delivered in September 1968 flew its entire career with the Bulgarian carrier, before scrapping in 1985 at Sofia. Seen here at Paris Orly in August 1979   **Jacques Barbé**

Interflug of East Germany operated Tu-134A DM-SCM from delivery in 1973 until a landing accident five years later at Berlin Schönefeld, caused by the improper use of the autopilot; no fatalities. Basel **Jacques Barbé**

it went into a deep stall, a threat to all aircraft with a high T-tail, in which, at a high angle of attack and low airspeed, the aircraft will not only stall but be irrecoverable due to the turbulent wash from the stalled wings blanking the effectiveness of the elevators, making the required nose-down recovery impossible.

The data shared by the British authorities to aircraft manufacturers around the world, regardless of political divisions, undoubtedly saved many lives and is to be applauded (and just a few years after they did the same with what they learned about metal fatigue after the Comet crashes.) The Tupolev OKB incorporated these essential new findings into the design of a new, bigger and more effective horizontal stabiliser, the first of which was retrofitted to CCCP-65600 along with D-30s and this upgraded prototype was flown on October 26, 1966.

These final design changes heralded the start of full production at factory no. 135, now renamed KhAZ, and Tu-134s began to appear on the production line sandwiched between late-build Tu-124s.

In June 1967 CCCP-65610 visited the 26th Paris Air Show, two years after the type's debut there. The Tu-134 was certified by the authorities on August 26, 1967 and on the same day CCCP-65600 operated a route-proving flight from Moscow to Murmansk with 23 passengers onboard.

The first revenue flight of a Tu-134 was operated by Aeroflot on September 9 from Moscow to the Black Sea resort city of Sochi with CCCP-656000. Due to its certification by the Montreal-headquartered International Civil Aviation Organisation (ICAO) at the same time, the Tu-134 was able to be used on international flights to European capital cities immediately (mostly displacing the propjet Ilyushin Il-18); the first international flight by the type was from Moscow to Stockholm on September 9, followed by Kiev to Vienna (originating in Moscow) on September 14 by CCCP-65606 and Moscow to Belgrade on September 16. On October 2, CCCP-65611 operated the first revenue Tu-134 flight into Warsaw, CCCP-65606 opened up Helsinki, and and CCCP-65610 was introduced on the Zurich run.

Aviaexport All Union Agency, the authority tasked with selling Soviet aircraft abroad, sent CCCP-65610 on an international sales tour to Japan where it arrived at Tokyo Haneda on October 21 and stayed for five days on display and operated

The cabin of a Perm Airlines TU-134A3, RA-65064 stored at Perm airport, Russia in 2014. **Simon De Rudder**

CCCP-65090, delivered to Aeroflot in January 1978, seen here at Simferopol, went on to fly for 13 years with KD Avia and another six years with Orenair, before going into storage at Orenburg in 2011 **B. Korzin** Transport-Photo Images

a number of short sectors for evaluation by Japan Air Lines and All Nippon Airways. CCCP-65610 also went to Hungary on November 21 where it spent three days demonstrating to Malev, then flew to Czechoslovakia on November 24 and spent three days demonstrating for CSA.

Balkan Bulgarian Airlines was chosen to be the first export customer partly due to the close relationship between Andrei Tupolev, who was the president of the Soviet-Bulgarian Society, and Tsola Dragoycheva, a formidable Bulgarian who was a guerrilla fighter against the Nazis in World War 2 and, since 1947, Bulgaria's first female cabinet member.

Three Tu-104s were delivered to Balkan's base at Sofia, starting with LZ-TUA and followed by TUB and TUC which were handed over still bearing the livery of the airline's previous identity, TABSO. London was the destination for the inaugural flight on November 11. On November 12, before its return trip to Sofia, LZ-TUA operated a 90-minute demonstration flight out of London Heathrow for the media who wrote glowing reports of the comfort and appeal of the modern jetliner.

Interflug, East Germany's national carrier, was next in line to receive the new jetliner, with DM-SCA arriving in September 1968 and SCB and SCD following in quick succession. The three machines were used for extensive crew training, followed by a demonstration flight operated on February 29, 1969 from Berlin to Leipzig for the famous Leipzig Trade Fair, and hence the passengers were mostly airline and travel executives including top brass from Aeroflot, CSA, TAROM, Sabena, British European Airways, SAS, TWA and Japan Air Lines. Interflug's first true revenue Tu-134 flight was to Beirut on April 2.

Another early export customer was Yugoslavian charter airline Aviogenex, who received three Tu-134s, YU-AHH and AHI in 1969 followed by AHS in early 1970. However even as further orders piled up from both Aeroflot and foreign carriers, Tupolev worked to improve the design. Early upgrades included a larger forward passenger entry door and replacement of the rotating anti-collision beacon with a brighter flashing beacon.

The first in a long line of redesignated variants came in the form of the Tu-134K, a standard Tu-134 with a VIP interior (K for Komfort). Four were used by the Soviet authorities for head of state transport; four also went to East Germany for their top brass, two to Hungary, one to Bulgaria and one to Iraq.

The first major upgrade to the baseline machine was the Tu-134A, which incorporated a 2.1 metre (6 feet 10 inches) stretch, most of which was used to expand the rear main deck baggage area which on the early Tu-134 *sans suffixe* was too small, and to add a single row of passenger seating.

Tu-134 *sans suffixe* slowed down after landing with the help of a braking parachute which had to be dropped onto the runway until a ground crew could go out and retrieve it, eating up runway capacity horribly. Instead, the upgraded Soloviev D-30s on the Tu-134A had reverse thrust (the two pilots had separate sets of throttles; only the captain's included the ability to command reverse thrust).

The engines on the Tu-134 *sans suffixe* were started by using electrical power from the battery, whereas the upgraded version for the Tu-134A had low-pressure air starters using the new TA-8 auxiliary power unit (APU), installed in the bay previously occupied by the braking chute. This also helped passenger comfort on the ground during very hot or very cold days, as it was able to provide climate control in the cabin. Other modifications included an improved fuel system which reduced the time needed for the engines to respond to throttle movements, more sophisticated cabin pressure controls, and a SEUZ-1 flap synchroniser to prevent asymmetric flap deployment.

The prototype Tu-134A was CCCP-65624, a regular Tu-134 that had the fuselage stretch plug inserted on the production line.

It first flew on April 22 (Lenin's birthday) in 1969, and on May 25 was exhibited at what was becoming the Tu-134's second home, the Paris Air Show, alongside a Tu-134 *sans suffixe* which was there for contrast to highlight the latest upgrades to the design. Route proving began with the first production models on the busy Moscow to Leningrad run in the spring of 1970, and the first revenue flight was on November 9. The Tu-134A went on to become the most produced variant, with over 400 built (including over 180 VIP Tu-134AKs).

Improvements continued to be added, small and large. The Tu-134 *sans suffixe* and early-build Tu-134As came with a large ventral spoiler that would extend downwards from under the wing box to enable an descent profile of up to nine degrees. With the increased use of ILS landing systems which standardised on an approach

YK-AYA was delivered to Syria in 1982 and is seen at Heathrow after a rainshower **Richard Vandervord**

Tu-134A VN-A104 served Hang Khonh Vietnam for its entire career on domestic and regional trips for the newly-reunited country, from February 1979 until retirement and scapping at Hanoi in 1996 **Christofer Witt**

Kishinev turnaround in the mid 1980s

Valentin Grebnev Transport-Photo Images

path of three degrees, the ventral spoiler was eliminated from March 1978 onwards (CCCP-65112 was the first to be constructed without it) and the device was locked closed on the rest of the Tu-134s. At the same time, flap travel was limited to 30 degrees (from 38) to reduce the forces applied to the flap drive jackscrews, and to reduce noise levels. Pilots initially complained – it was said that with the ventral spoiler extended and full flap, the aircraft would land itself. (Perhaps another way of putting that would be to say, with that much drag, the aircraft would be incapable of sustaining flight!)

Early Tu-134s including A models were fitted with a glass nose for a navigator, and an ROZ-1 'chin' radar (a blister fairing under the nose), however, at the behest of foreign operators, the Tupolev OKB created a three-crew cockpit with the new Groza-M134 weather radar installed in the nose, which was now opaque. The prototype of the new configuration was YU-AHX, the first of several ordered by Aviogenex, delivered after flight trials in March 1971. Because of Aviogenex's role in developing this evolution, the radar-nosed Tu-134As were often known in the Eastern Bloc as 'the Yugoslav version', and more correctly as the Tu-134A-1. They also had larger rear emergency exits to satisfy the British Civil Airworthiness Regulations, who insisted on the change as Aviogenex were doing a lot of flying to and from the UK. The East German government were also a keen customer for the Tu-134AK-1, adding eight to their government fleet in addition to the original four Tu-134Ks.

More upgrades: the Tu-134A-3 was basically a Tu-134A-1 with uprated D-30 engines (the D-30-III) although some machines intended to be A-3s were downgraded to A-1s due to production hiccups with the latest Solvievs.

Despite the reputation of Soviet aviation for being a rather austere customer experience, inflight entertainment was tried on Leningrad-based Tu-134s on the busy run to Moscow, with ten TV sets suspended from the overhead hat racks of their fleet in early 1971. It was decided that big TV sets flying around in a crash landing could turn an otherwise survivable event into a deadly one, and the trial was not extended to other fleets.

A more sophisticated addition was the ABSU-134 autoland system which allowed ICAO Cat II landings with a decision height of 330 feet (100 metres) and forward visibility of 1,300 feet (400 metres). CCCP-65966, a Tupolev-owned flying avionics testbed since birth, was used by

YL-LBA spent the 1980s at Aeroflot and most of the 1990s with Latavio flying out Riga, followed by 15 years starting at the turn of the century with Alrosa, finally retired in 2015
Guy Van Herbruggen

GosNII GA by Captain Viktor Ilyich Shkatov in a test programme that began on August 22, 1973 and lasted nearly three years. The new system was finally certified on March 20, 1976 and became fitted as standard on all Tu-134s from the end of July 1977 onwards, starting with Tu-134AK CCCP-65073.

Interflug requested an upgraded autoland system due to Berlin's famously poor winter weather of low ceilings and fog. DM-SCM was fitted with a BSU-3P autoland system upgraded by replacing some modules of the avionics system, giving a lowered decision height of 150 feet (45 metres) and reduced forward visibility of 1,300 feet (400 metres), but the aircraft crashed on November 22, 1977 at Berlin Schönefeld airport when the autoland system was misused, resulting in an excessive sink rate of seven metres per second (nearly 1,400 feet per minute). With the left wing torn off and the landing gear gone, the fuselage skidded for 400 metres but luckily none of the 74 on board lost their lives.

The early years of Tu-134 operation were notable for being very safe, especially as the Tu-104's aerodynamic quirks had been ironed out of the wing, although the record was marred by some crashes due to pilot error. On May 23, 1971, Aviogenex's YU-AHZ crashed on landing at Rijeka after a flight from London Gatwick due to a high sink rate, with the only survivors being the four cockpit crew and one passenger. On September 16 of the same year, Malev's HA-LBD crashed on landing at Kiev after two missed approaches with an electrical failure adding a layer of complication, with the loss of all 49 onboard. East German authorities jailed the flight crew of DM-SCD for negligence after getting too low and too slow to avoid hitting an antenna short of the runway at Leipzig on September 1, 1975, a crash which killed 27 of the 34 onboard. September 21, 1977 saw Malev lose HA-LBC in another landing accident caused by pilot error, this time in Bucharest, with the loss of 29 onboard; 24 survived.

Despite the frequency of accidents, these were not reflective of the Tu-134 or Soviet aviation overall, at least by the standards of the era. Airlines in the West endured a similar toll – for instance, Pan Am suffered four fatal 707 crashes between December 1968 and April 1974 with the loss of 333 souls, three of which took place in a single nine month period. Ground-based navigation aids, cockpit procedures, behavioural factors and the hardware, state-of-the-art though it was for the time,

■ RA-65038 leads a line up of Tyumen Airlines Tu-134As; this particular frame was delivered to Aeroflot in November 1976 and today is displayed in Aeroflot colours at Borovaya in Belarus **Richard Vandervord**

■ Tu-134 cockpit **Alex Beltyukov**

■ 1980-build Tu-134A RA-65579 in the colourful livery of Dagestan Airlines **Richard Vandervord**

■ This Tu-134 was built as a B-1 in 1981 and remained with the Tupolev design bureau who later converted it to a B-3; in 1992 it migrated to Russia's FSB secret police, and later to Georgia where it became UR-BYY **Richard Vandervord**

simply hadn't evolved to today's levels where even with the massive increase in traffic, accidents are far rarer.

A new designation, the Tu-134B, represented a leap forward to cockpit ergonomics, introducing at last a central control pedestal between the two pilots where previously there had been a gap for the navigator to squeeze forward into his glass nose, and later, the radar display. The console was used for throttles, flap and spoiler controls and radios. Passenger accommodation was increased to 80 by reducing the size of the forward luggage hold and shrinking the galley. Inflatable emergency exit slides replaced canvas slides.

Prototype Tu-134B CCCP-65146 was completed in late 1979 and went into flight trials on March 31, 1980. The first production aircraft, CCCP-65799, followed on April 30, and 32 more were built,

Tu-134AK D2-ECC served the government of Angola from April 1977 until at least July 2006 but possibly as late as October 2014
Richard Vandervord

plus 14 of the VIP version, designated Tu-134B-3s, some of which were exported to Bulgaria (two), Vietnam and Syria (three each).

In April 1983 an increased capacity variant was attempted, the prototype for which was CCCP-65966, a joint venture between KhAPO in Kharkov, the Tupolev OKB in Moscow and ARZ no. 407, the maintenance facility at Minsk-1 which specialised in heavy checks and other work on the Tu-134 (and Yakovlev Yak-40). The first 16 rows featured five abreast seating in a very tight 2-3 arrangement, with the three rows in the rear cabin in the style of the previous 2-2 arrangement. At the request of Aeroflot, the navigator's station with a glazed nose was back, but the larger exits of the Tu-134A-1 were retained. Despite the increased seating reducing trip costs by 18%, the price in terms of sacrificed passenger comfort was considered to be too great, and the project was abandoned.

The Tu-134 proved to be an extraordinarily versatile platform for the wide range of missions required by a country spanning 11 time zones and covering a sixth of the world's land surface. One such role was crop surveying and geophysical experiments performed by the Tu-134SKh variant, all nine of which were initially based at Voronezh, based on the Tu-134A-3 and put into service on September 28, 1984 after a year of test flying by CCCP-65917, and were used to measure soil humidity, detect the presence of pests, and assess crop yield. The cabin was filled with scientific measuring equipment and the main exterior feature were the two podded eight-metre (26 feet 3 inch) antennae under the wing roots which housed side-looking radar (SLAR). Other Tu-134SKh roles included service to the oil and gas extraction industry, to the fisheries of Kamchatka, as an ice reconnaissance platform in the Arctic, as a forestry inspection vehicle, and as an ore finder.

Some specific missions involving the Tu-134SKh included the Aral-88 expedition which surveyed the rapidly shrinking (and now completely gone) Aral Sea; in 1989 to assess the damage after the December 7, 1988 earthquake that devastated Armenia, detecting potential landslide areas and damaged irrigation facilitates which could cause floods if ruptured; and in 1990 extensive work around Leningrad to assess the environmental damage done by a dam project that had polluted the Neva Bight. In 1992, the Tu-134SKh took part in the PECHERI Russian-US hydrological experiment alongside Douglas DC-8 and Lockheed Orion aircraft, as well as the Russian oceanological research ship MV Academic Ioffe, and the ERS-1 satellite.

■ Ice on the window during Alrosa flight 542 from Irkutsk to Mirny in January 2018 **Simon De Rudder**

■ Sirius Aero Tu-134B-3 RA-65700 was originally delivered to the USSR air force in 1983 **Artyom Kuzhlev**

■ Marsland Aviation operated ST-MRS in Sudan for eight years starting in 2003 before passing her on to Dove Air for another five years of flying Sudanese skies   **Richard Vandervord**

■ Air Koryo's P-814 was the second of two Tu-134B-3s delivered to North Korea's flag carrier   **Bernie Leighton**

The military saw the value of the Tu-134 early on, and the Tu-134Sh, NATO reporting name Crusty-A, was a navigation trainer that emerged as early as January 1971; the first aircraft was designated Red 01. The first batch were known as Tu-134Sh-1 and were mostly used by the Chelyabinsk Military Navigator College in central Russia, and the Combat and Conversion Training Centre at Dyaghilevo air base at Ryazan, southeast of Moscow. The interior contained twelve workstations for trainee navigators who graduated to flying the Tupolev Tu-22 Blinder and Tu-22M2 and M3 Backfire strategic bombers. The Tu-134Sh-2, NATO reporting name Short Horn, followed in January 1972 and was used to train navigators for tactical bombers such as the Yakovlev Yak-28 Brewer and Sukhoi Su-24 Fencer. Some Tu-134Sh aircraft were later converted to VIP aircraft in service with the navy, and one was used for ferrying cosmonauts between the Chkalovskaya air base and the Baikonour space centre.

There were several variants specifically developed as part of the Soviet space programme, most notably a fleet of Tu-134LKs based at 70th Independent Special Test and Training Air Regiment in Chkalovskaya in May 1980. These were used to train Soviet and foreign cosmonauts who flew missions to the Salyut-6, Salyut-7 and Mir space stations. An important contribution to the Buran ('snowstorm') space shuttle was the

Meridian Air Tu-134B-3 RA-65737 was originally delivered to the USSR air force in 1982   Artyom Kuzhlev

the autoland equipment that allowed it to fly unmanned; this was developed using CCCP-65931, a one-off calibrator testbed based mostly on the Tu-134B and known as the Tu-134BV.

1983 saw another single-frame designation, the Tu-134IK, built for the Soviet Ministry Of Defence, bristling with antennae and almost certainly used in relation to the space programme (IK refers to the Russian for measurement suite).

The most distinctive military variant was the Tu-134UBL, NATO reporting name Crusty-B. It was a trainer for the Tu-160 Blackjack as well as Tu-22M2 and M3 bombers. The hot rod bombers had limited service lives due to the sensitivity of their engines, yet the Tu-134 had a similar thrust-to-weight ratio and low-speed handling characteristics. In addition there was no dedicated trainer version of those bombers, so Tu-134Bs were adapted with a very long pointed nose adding 4.7 metres (16 feet) to the length of the aircraft, adopted straight off the Tu-22. The cockpit panels were changed to resemble the Tu-22M, and three rows of passenger seats were installed in the forward passenger cabin for 12 trainees to sit awaiting their chance to fly. Parachutes were fitted and the rear cargo door had a powerful pneumatic arm that could open it inflight to permit the crew to bail out in an emergency.

The first Tu-134UBL prototype was CCCP-64010 which was manufactured in January 1981. By July 24 the needle-nosed variant was cleared for service. Trials with a second prototype, CCCP-64020, included spin recovery tests with an emergency spin recovery parachute on an arm extending out behind the tail, and were completed in June 1982. Initial deliveries were to Engels-2 air base near Saratov in April 1981, and by the time production of the Tu-134 ended in 1983, 90 were built, including 35 in 1982 alone. Most were used for pilot training or weapons system trainers and avionics testbeds. A sole example was used by the navy and designated Tu-134UBK.

The last production aircraft were rolled out in September 1984, mostly Tu-134AK Salon machines with a few final Tu-134Bs for export customers such as Air Koryo, Syrianair and Vietnam Airlines. After that, machines were made to order for five more years. The last passenger-configured was Tu-134AK registered XU-102 which rolled off the line at Kharkov on December 15, 1986, and the last of any kind was Tu-104SKh crop surveyer CCCP-65723 on June 30, 1989. Total production was 852 plus two prototypes, an impressive total which brought jet aviation to the masses in a huge chunk of the Eurasian landmass as well as being an export success.

With the break-up of the Soviet Union into Russia and a Commonwealth of Independent States (CIS), national airlines popped up using the equipment that was at hand, and independent airlines within Russia sprang to life. Hundreds of Aeroflot Tu-134s were hurriedly repainted in the livery of flag carriers for fledging nations, symbols of private enterprise in a region that had been stolidly communist only months earlier.

Throughout the 1990s, Russia and her neighbours' fleets of Tu-134s provided essential air links to communities large and small, just as they had during the Soviet Union, albeit in the old days they all wore the livery of Aeroflot, and after the breakup a countless number of colour schemes and brands emerged, some little more than new titles (or none at all) over Aeroflot cheatlines, others colourful and imaginative new brands to wow newly-mobile Russians, Kazakhs, Armenians, and other former citizens of the socialist bloc. Some Tu-134s migrated to exotic climes, such as Harka Air in Nigeria and Marsland in Sudan.

The safety record remained excellent in the post-Soviet era but nonetheless it was an accident that brought the career of the Tu-134 to an end with Aeroflot, when UTAir's flight 671 crashed on landing at Samara on March 17, 2007. Although the cause was pilot error, Russia's national airline felt the accident was a sign that the now-elderly workhorse's time was up, and operated their last trip with the type on January 1, 2008.

On June 20, 2011, RusAir 9605 ran low on fuel and attempted to land on a road; the crash killed 47 passengers and crew. Technical problems in the cockpit hindered the crew's performance and the Russian authorities ordered that all Tu-134s be removed from commercial service by the last day of the same year.

Today a handful of Tu-134s fly on – Air Koryo have both of their 1984-build machines still working, mostly on short domestic hops within North Korea. A handful remain flying as passenger liners in provincial Russia. The Tu-134UBL trainers are as busy as ever and a few VIP conversions, popular in the 90s with newly-minted Russian superrich, fly on. With examples of the type still airborne every day more than 50 years after the first flight of the prototype, the Tu-134 is a proven workhorse of the skies.

A governmental Tu-134A-3 RA-65911 getting pulled out for a training flight from Moscow Vnukovo in July 2016
Simon De Rudder

B. Kozin Transport-Photo Images

Ilyushin Il-62
The flagship

The Soviet Union had a jetliner (the Tu-104) and a long hauler (the Tu-114 propliner) but it took the Il-62 to be both, bringing the most far-flung corners of the empire, and the world, to Moscow at jet speed.

The story of Russia's first long haul jetliner begins in the century before last, with the birth of aircraft designer Sergei Vladimirovich Ilyushin on March 30, 1894, in the Vologda Oblast in northeast Russia. After training in the Tsarist Army as a pilot in 1917, and as an aircraft technician in the Red Army after the revolution, his future as one of the world's most famous aircraft designers was probably set in stone in late 1919 when a British Avro 504 fighter plane crashed near Petrozavodsk – he was one of the team who took the plane apart and transported it to Moscow to be reverse-engineered as the Soviet U-1 trainer, of which 707 were built. In 1921 Ilyushin joined the Red Army Engineering Institute and the Air Force Science and Technical Committee in 1926. In 1931 he began working as an aircraft designer at TsAGI, and in 1933 became chief designer at the TsKB (Ts = Central, KB = Design Bureau) which in 1935 became the Ilyushin OKB.

The first production aircraft designed by the Ilyushin OKB was the Il-2 ground attack aircraft which was then the most produced aircraft of all time, with 36,183 built (including the Il-10 development, the number rises to 42,330). After World War 2, the focus turned to civil aviation – between 1950 and 1959, domestic air traffic within the Soviet Union grew tenfold. The Ilyushin OKB was at the forefront, with the first of 2,011 Il-12 and Il-14 propliners flying in 1950, and the four-engined long haul Ilyushin Il-18 turboprop following in 1957.

The Tupolev Tu-104 was doing great work and could stay up for two or three hours at a time, but the Soviet Union needed a true long haul machine, so in February 1960 Sergei Ilyushin himself presented a proposal for a four-engined passenger jet to the Soviet Council Of Ministers, and received a formal go-ahead on June 18. The Kuznetsov OKB, specialising in aeroengines, was simultaneously instructed to develop what would become the NK-8 turbofan engine.

The placement of the engines in pairs on the rear fuselage would later be controversial in the West as it so closely replicated the contemporary Vickers VC-10 produced in Britain. In fact the configuration was dictated by TsAGI on the basis that the Ilyushin OKB did not have the resources to engage in prolonged configuration studies and engine placement on the rear fuselage was considered scientifically correct and thus immutable. (Indeed engines attached to the wing by pylons remained anathema to Soviet airline design until the entry into service of the widebody Ilyushin Il-86 in 1980.)

The layout was also shared with the Lockheed L-329 / L-1329 Jetstar business jet, against which there are no accusations of plagiarism, and has several advantages which are no doubt why it appealed to Vickers and Lockheed as well as Ilyushin – a very quiet passenger cabin, a clean wing optimised for aerodynamic efficiency, and a smaller rudder required due to the lack of asymmetrical thrust in the event of an engine failure.

Another noteworthy design element on the Il-62 is the distinctive 'dogtooth' indentation in the leading edge of the wing, which was added to create a powerful vortex over the wing at low speeds, localising the turbulent airflow of an incipient aerodynamic stall and protecting the high lift outboard wing. The flight controls were fitted with a 'stick shaker' to warn of an approaching aerodynamic stall, and a 'stick pusher' to physically force the control column forward if the aircraft reached a fully-stalled condition. This feature was met by resistance by pilots at the time, but is a feature of all T-tailed aircraft today.

The horizontal stabiliser is small for the size of the aircraft and the consequent aerodynamic load. This reduces cruise drag significantly (and structural weight a bit) at the expense of having the wing placed slighty further forward. This creates no issues in flight but in some loading regimes, can place the centre of gravity aft of the main landing gear, which gave rise to another Il-62 trademark, the retractable tail stand extended when the aircraft is parked. With the tail stand in place, loading and unloading can be done in any order without risk of the aircraft tipping up on its tail.

The first prototype, registered CCCP-06156, taxied under its own power at Khodynka airfield in Moscow, on September 19, 1962. The engines used initially were Ljulka AL-7 turbojets as the Kuznetsov NK-8 was still being readied for use. The AL-7 had many successful military applications such as the Sukhoi Su-7 Fitter and Su-9 Fishpot as well as the AS-3 Kangaroo cruise missile and even the Beriev Be-10 flying boat.

CCCP-06156 was formally unveiled to the country's top brass including General Secretary Nikita Khrushchev at Khodynka on September 24. After that, the machine was dismantled and transported by road to Zhukovsky, south east of the capital, home of TsAGI and the Soviet Union's main centre of aerospace research and development, where it was reassembled for flight testing. High

■ Il-62 at the 1973 Paris Air Show

Piergiuliano Chesi

speed taxi runs resumed on December 19, and the aircraft even made a few short hops into the air of a few seconds each.

The Il-62's first flight was a successful 34 minute sortie on the morning of January 2, 1963 under the command of Captain Vladimir K. Kokkinaki, joined by First Officer Eduard I Kuznetsov, navigator V. F. Voskresenkiy, flight engineer I. B. Kuss, radio operator V. S. Siliminov, and project engineer P. V. Kazakov. A second prototype, CCCP-06153, was transported to Zhukovsky and after reassembly flew with Kuznetsov NK-8 engines on April 24, and also had redesigned ailerons for better roll control.

The Il-62 test programme suffered a major blow when, on February 25 1965, CCCP-06156 crashed at the start of its 127th flight. Under the command of Captain A. S. Lipko, during a maximum takeoff weight test, CCCP-06156 lifted off with a high angle-of-attack and low airspeed, and, unable to gain altitude, hit the airfield perimeter fence before crashing in the countryside beyond, with the loss of 10 of the 17 men onboard, three of whom (navigator Voskresenskiy, flight engineer Kuss and test engineer Kazakov) had been on the first flight.

Undaunted, a third prototype, CCCP-06176, made its way to Zhukovsky for a first flight on July 28, and production began at the famous Aircraft Factory Number 22 in Kazan, Tatarstan; CCCP-06170 and -06300, the first two production aircraft, joined the test programme on route-proving trials. On May 11, Captain Boris A. Anapov commanded a ten hour flight that covered 8,050 km (5,000 miles), and on July 9, flew the ship in an airshow at Moscow Domodedovo airport, leading a column of commercial aircraft in the display which unveiled the Soviet Union's new flagship to the public. On July 11, another Kazan-built machine, CCCP-86666, left Moscow and overflew Murmansk, the North Pole, and Sverdlovsk (today Yekaterinburg) before returning to base, covering 8,940 km (5,556 miles) in ten hours and 48 minutes;

the purpose of the sortie was to check the avionics for navigation accuracy.

CCCP-86661 was the first production aircraft to be fully civilianised, with the anti-spin parachute in the tail replaced by a TA-6 auxiliary power unit, and was delivered to Aeroflot's base at Krasnoyarsk in Siberia. The first Il-62 revenue flight was performed on September 8, 1967 on the trunk route from Moscow to the Kazakh republic's capital city of Alma Ata (today Almaty). The following week saw the Il-62 make its international debut, displacing the Tu-114 propliner from the transatlantic route to Montreal. The triumph and tragedy of the four-year test programme had paid off.

The first export customer for the Il-62 was Czechoslovakia's flag carrier CSA, who got their first machine, OK-YBA, on October 29, 1969, followed by -YBB on November 28 for services to Moscow and a long-haul to Jakarta via Damascus, Karachi and Rangoon (today Yangon). (As a star pupil of the Warsaw Pact airlines, CSA had been the first airline after Aeroflot to fly the Tu-104, and was even in the frame to operate the supersonic Tu-144 in the late 1970s.)

East Germany's national carrier Interflug was next, DM-SEA arriving at Berlin Schönefeld

Four Interflug Il-62Ms at Berlin Schönefeld   IF 810

■ Classic Il-62 CCCP-86680 taxies at Paris Le Bourget on May 13, 1970 **Jacques Barbé**

■ A pair of Il-62s in the hangar at Domodedovo in the mid 1970s **Valentin Grebnev** Transport-Photo Images

on Lenin's 100th birthday, April 22, 1970 to begin service to Moscow, followed by the Middle East – Cairo, Baghdad, Damascus, and later as far afield as Dubai, Tashkent, Havana, Hanoi, Lagos, Luanda, Karachi, Maputo and Singapore, as well as intra-European sectors such as Amsterdam, Prague, Athens and Paris.

Further export customers included the CAAC (Civil Aviation Administration Of China) and United Arab Airlines / Egyptair in 1971, TAROM of Romania and Cubana in 1972, and LOT Polish Airlines in 1973. Air France and Japan Air Lines both wet-leased Il-62s from Aeroflot for service to Russia and Japan, carrying dual titles in the Aeroflot livery.

Mostly they were used on long haul trips – LOT put theirs straight into transatlantic service from Warsaw to New York, Toronto and Chicago serving the large Polish populations there, while TAROM initially used theirs on shorter trips but made it across the Atlantic in the end, to New York and Chicago, with a tech stop in Amsterdam.

A suggested modification to improve range was designated the Il-62D (D for Dahl'niy – "long range" in Russian), which involved using the rear of the main deck for additional fuel tanks; Sergei Ilyushin felt this was not ideal for either safety or efficiency, and instead worked towards the Il-62M (M for modifitseerovannyy – "modified"), the most important upgrade being the use of Soloviev D-30 engines, which were turbofans with a higher bypass ratio than the NK-8, a better engine nacelle, lower exterior noise, and a new clamshell reverse thrust bracket.

Other upgrades were the addition of a 5,000 litre tank in the tail fin, asymmetric spoiler control to assist the ailerons in roll, refined elevators for better pitch control, an upgraded APU, better cockpit lighting, new control yokes and ICAO category II-compliant avionics.

After 94 standard Il-62s were delivered, production switched to the Il-62M, the first example, CCCP-86656, getting into the air on April 15, 1972. Test flying was extensive and even included a

trip to South America to evaluate the aircraft's performance at "hot and high" airfields. The certification process was complete by November 1973 and the first revenue service with Aeroflot took place on January 8, 1974.

Most of the airlines who operated the original Il-62 took the M version, mostly in a one-for-one fleet upgrade. Three new export customers were found – TAAG Angola (two aircraft were delivered, D2-TIF and -TIG), DETA Mozambique (one aircraft, registered C9-BAE), and Choson Minhang (today Air Koryo) of North Korea, who took four passenger liners and a head of state Salon aircraft.

After the success of the Il-62M, a few further variants were produced in very small numbers, such as the Il-62MK, a shorter range version intended for high frequency short range operations (sixteen for Aeroflot and two for Interflug); and the Il-62MU, a combi (just one, RA-86586, operated by the Kazan factory's own airline, KAPO Avia). The Il-62M-250 was a stretched variant, boasting an extra 22 feet and 3 inches (6.8 metres), but never left the drawing board.

While the Il-62 had an excellent safety record, with only a handful of fatal accidents, LOT

Polish Airlines' experience was noteworthy for the loss of two aircraft in identical accidents at Warsaw, seven years apart. LO 007, operated by SP-LAA, the first Il-62 delivered to the airline, was landing after an overnight flight from New York on the morning of March 14, 1980, when it initiated a go-around due to a landing gear warning light. Upon the application of full power, engine number two engine exploded, cutting control lines to the tail and causing an immediate uncontrollable descent into the ground just outside the airport perimeter with the loss of all 87 on board.

In an eery repetition, on May 9, 1987, SP-LBG, a Il-62M, was operating LO 5055 to New York. Climbing hard to comply with an air traffic control instruction to avoid a block of military airspace in its path, number two engine exploded, taking out engine number one and all of the flight controls except pitch trim, and starting a fire in the rear cargo hold. Remarkably, the crew were able to keep the disabled machine in the air for 31 minutes and nearly made it back to the runway at Warsaw, but in the end the ship was unflyable and crashed at the opposite end of the airport from the 1980 tragedy, taking with it a further 183 lives.

In the wake of the second accident, LOT pioneered some safety upgrades to the Il-62, including duplication of flight control systems, replacing flammable elements in the cargo hold, installation of smoke detectors, and upgraded engine vibration detection systems and fire detection systems.

While 1989 itself was bad, with two major crashes (Interflug due to pilot error and Cubana due to windshear), the two decades that followed, which were the years with the most Il-62s flying, were notable for seeing no fatal accidents. Compared to the 707, VC10 and DC-8, the Il-62 had the lowest incidence of accidents, with 22 fatal accidents and a further 11 aircraft written off without fatalities.

Although the country that created the Il-62, the Soviet Union, had ceased to exist, the 1990s were in many ways the Il-62's halcyon era, as the deregulation of the Russian airline scene saw the splintering of an industry that was up to that point sedate and top heavy into new flag carriers as

■ Il-62 SP-LAE Henryk Sienkiewicz of LOT Polish Airlines at Milan Malpensa in April 1975 went to Aeroflot 1984 to 1993, and to Kras Air 1993 to 2003 when it was scrapped locally in Krasnoyarsk **Jacques Barbé**

Interflug Il-62 postcard

Aeroflot Il-62 promotional photo from the early 1970s

Air Kokshetau Il-62 safety card

The start of an eight hour trip to Moscow is boarding at Vladivostok; this Il-62M served Aeroflot its entire life from April 1978 until May 1996
Valentin Grebnev Transport-Photo Images

the former Soviet republics became independent nations. What had previously been Aeroflot's Uzbek base at Tashkent became Uzbekistan Airlines, inheriting a fleet of four Il-62 and eleven Il-62Ms to begin serving cities as far afield as London and Seoul. Air Ukraine, previously Aeroflot's Kiev operation, sprang to life with seven Il-62Ms and opened up transatlantic flights to New York and Toronto in one direction, Bangkok in the other.

In the Russian domestic scene, new independent airlines multiplied – Interavia, Aviaenergo, Dalavia, SAT, and VIM all flew large fleets of the Il-62 in the 1990s. 45 machines passed through the hands of Domodedovo Airlines alone. At most of these airlines, the ageing Il-62s were flown hard enough to peel the paint off – some averaged 17 hours of use per day. In the Czech Republic, ex-CSA machines were snapped up cheaply by budding airline moguls to create Espe Air Prague, Egret BMI and Bemoair.

Aeroflot itself, while a fraction of its former size, was able to benefit from the reduction in political tension -- the peace dividend - in the world, and catered to increased international flying. New routes were added including Moscow-Larnaca-Sal-Rio-Sao Paolo, and Moscow-Shannon-Havana-Panama-Managua. In fact the Il-62M fleet was doing so much transatlantic flying that on certain days of the week, eight aircraft were dropping into Shannon for refuelling in the space of a few hours – each way.

An interesting aside to the Il-62 and Aeroflot's story with Shannon: starting in the 1980s, Aeroflot (after moving some of their stopover traffic to Gander in Canada due to high fuel prices at Shannon) came to an arrangement with the handling agent at Shannon. The Soviet Union, and later Russia, could build their own fuel farm and deliver their own fuel to the airport. This fuel was supplied by the Russian government. By the mid 1980s, 3,000 Aeroflot movements a year were being fueled, with regular deliveries of 1.25 million gallons of top quality Jet A-1 on tankers from the Black Sea. For Aeroflot, the pleasing collateral benefit of this arrangement was that as the fuel came from their government, it somehow didn't show up on Aeroflot's financials. So the story goes, Aer Rianta then offered Aeroflot free landing fees and ground handling services (parking, steps, ground power, line maintenance etc) in return for the ability to sell off some of this magic free fuel to other airlines just a little less than at market rate. This made the airport a popular stopover and attracted TWA, Rich International, American Trans Air, Worldways and TAROM on their way to and from the Atlantic. Hey, get a little, give a little.

As the 1990s rolled into the 2000s, the availability of middle-aged Boeing and Airbus jets

Il-62 turnaround at Petropavlovsk

B. Korzin Transport-Photo Images

■ A trio of Air Ukraine Il-62Ms serving long haul routes out of Kiev through the 1990s including Toronto, New York and Bangkok
Sergey Popsuevich Transport-Photo Images

■ Cubana's Il-62M CU-T1209 was delivered factory fresh from Kazan to Havana on January 18 1978 and retired on June 30 1996 and scrapped
Richard Vandervord

■ Domodedovo Airport's eponymous airline fleet await their next mission **Pavel Novikov** Transport-Photo Images

The classic engine view from the back row of an Il-62 — Sam Chui

The wheelhouse of Air Koryo's P-885 between voyages — Jan Heistermann

LAM Mozambique was one of the Il-62's many export customers, with C9-BAE seen at Heathrow — **Richard Vandervord**

This Il-62M was delivered to Interflug in 1985 and went to Uzbekistan Airways as UK-86576 in the 1990s, and remains in service today as a freighter with Rada Airlines as EW-450TR — **Charles Bargibant**

Russian government Il-62M delivered in 1992 — **Artyom Kuzhlev**

with comparable seating capacity but superior economics finally spelled out a gradual end for the Il-62 and other Soviet-era hardware. Aeroflot's last 13 Il-62s were stood down on November 1, 2001. Other Russian carriers followed suit as the decade wore on. A common sight in provincial Russian airports for a while was old Ilyushins and Tupolevs parked around the fringes of the fields, streaked with mildew, birds nests in engine cowlings. Today most have been scrapped.

The final production Il-62 was built in 1995 without a delivery customer and put into storage. KAPO, the Kazan Aircraft Production Association, the latter-day owner of Aircraft Factory Number 22, formed KAPO Avia in 1999 and put RA-86586 into service themselves, flying charter trips or leases on behalf of some of the world's most obscure airlines – Magma Airlines, BGB Air, Luk Aero – before it was acquired by Kazakh broker Sayat Air and reregistered as UP-i6205.

The rock-bottom price and long range of the Il-62M, many of which were still available with low airframe hours, and with plenty of old boys who knew how to fly them still around (whose more adaptable, English-speaking erstwhile colleagues had gone off and by hook or by crook got themselves A320 and 737 typeratings and jobs with the emergent national carrier) were quite happy to drag their old Aeroflot uniform out of the closet in Almaty or Osh and go and fly Il-62s in Iran, Sudan or Equatorial Guinea.

Iran in particular represented rich pickings for airliners with pilots for hire, as documented in more detail in the chapter about the Tupolev Tu-154, as the country, geographically vast and with a huge and growing population, was restricted from buying new planes due to a diplomatic falling-out with the United States. Kazakh-sourced and –crewed Il-62s were brought in by Aria Air, but alas UP-i6208, delivered to Interflug in 1989, crashed on landing in Mashhad on July 24, 2009, which brought Aria Air's experiment to a premature end. For fans of the Il-62 this is a lost alternate future – Aria had big plans for the Il-62, with a fourth ship, UP-i6210, arriving from Kazakhstan to Tehran just eight days before the crash in the partial livery of previous operator InvestAvia, never to enter service with Aria Air. Expansion was not only planned to a wider Iranian domestic network, but international flights to Kuwait, Moscow, Istanbul,

▪ This late-build 1995 vintage Il-62M flew for Orient Avia as RA-86126 and today carries cargo for Manas Airways; isn't it odd to see such an old jet with a web address on the side?
Artyom Kuzhlev

P-885 was North Korea's first Il-62M and remains in service with Air Koryo today — Bernie Leighton

Drinks and meals are served aboard Air Koryo on the short sector from Beijing to Pyongyang — Sam Chui

North Korean leader Kim Jong Un's plane leaving   KCNA

Kim Jong Un aboard his head of state Il-62M   KCNA

and Bombay, with more Il-62s to come. UP-i6205's ferry flight to Fujairah in 2014 will almost certainly be its last, with only a thousand hours at most in the logbook – such is the price of being born too late.

Cubana was one of the last major airlines to fly the Il-62, with transatlantic flights (to Madrid, Paris, Frankfurt and Las Palmas) and routes throughout Latin and South America gradually being reduced to neighbouring Santo Domingo, Mexico City, Recife and Caracas. The last aircraft, CU-T1284, was stood down on March 1, 2011.

The following year, North Korea's flag carrier Air Koryo bought CU-T1280, reregistered it P-886P and in July 2012 flew it from Havana to Pyongyang where it was scrapped for parts to support North Korea's surviving pair of passenger machines (P-881 and P-885) plus Kim Jong Un's head of state aircraft ('Air Force Un'). Having once flown as far afield as Moscow, Berlin, Sofia and Belgrade in the halcyon days of the 1980s, by 2012 Air Koryo mainly flew the Il-62 on the trunk route to Beijing, with occasional appearances at Shenyang, Moscow, Bangkok and Macau. On the last day of 2012, China banned the type due to noise; P-881 went to the air force as a back-up for Air Force Un, leaving P-885, North Korea's first Il-62M (delivered in 1979), to remain in service.

Even in a country such as North Korea with a tiny geographical footprint, an economy operating (at least on face value) at a very low level, a population unable to travel, and the type banned on the main international trunk route (Beijing), there is still room for P-885 to make a living, as uplift is occasionally needed on ad hoc domestic runs (such as to transport a delegation to Mount Pektu, or a workers charter between Pyongyang and the country's second biggest city, the industrial hub of Hamhung). Air Koryo's once-a-week flight to Vladivostok, when demand outstrips the supply of seats on the usual Il-18, is subbed with the Il-62, which has no environmental restrictions against it in Russia. Don't dream it's over.

One more Il-62 was built, over a whole decade later – on October 8, 2009, RA-86495 was completed using parts at Kazan for the Russian government. Oddly, it was given the same

■ Investavia's UN-86130 (later UP-i6210) Il-62M is airborne out of Phuket at the start of the long trip back to Almaty   **Sam Chui**

manufacturer's serial number and registration as a 1977-build Il-62MK that flew for Aeroflot and the Soviet military and later with Moscow Airlines; that original machine was damaged beyond repair in 2002 and scrapped at Chkalovsky. The second incarnation of RA-86495 remains in service to this day with the Russian Air Force's 223rd Flight Unit which specialises in transport and logistics up to and including head of state transportation.

Comparison to the VC-10 is inevitable given the similar appearance of the two aircraft, and western chauvinism insists that the Vickers machine must be superior to the "VC-10ski", but while the VC-10 had inferior range and only 54 were produced, Russia's first long range jet was a success by any standard – 295 produced between 1963 and 1995 (plus 2009's one-off), flying for countless airlines in over 30 nations including 213 passing through the fleet of Aeroflot. Today the Il-62 remains in service with one airline (North Korea's Air Koryo) and a number of governments including Sudan, Russia, The Gambia and Ukraine. Of all the aircraft designed by Sergei Ilyushin, it is the silhouette of an Il-62 that is carved into his headstone as his greatest achievement – the flagship of the Soviet Union.

■ Delivered to Interflug in 1989 as DDR-SEY; Kazakh outfit DETA leased it to Aria Air as UP-i6208 in 2009, crashed in Mashhad July 2 **Guy Van Herbruggen**

■ Forty-Eight Airlines ran this 1990-build Il-62M on domestic flights in Sudan in 2011, now stored on the outskirts of Khartoum airport **Eduard Onyshchenko**

■ This 1986-build ex-Interflug Il-62M became UK-86575 serving a number of Uzbek carriers until scrapped at Moscow Domodedovo in October 2009 where it it is seen on July 4, 2005 **Richard Vandervord**

Fyodor Borisov Transport-Photo Images

Tupolev Tu-144
The Soviet SST

The world's first, heaviest and biggest supersonic airliner took to the skies on the last day of 1968 and six months later, on June 5 1969, accelerated through the sound barrier for the first time. The machine in question is not Concorde.

The 1960s was an age of technocratic futurism in the Soviet Union, flush with the success of Sputnik, the world's first space satellite in 1958, followed by the Vostok spaceflight programme that was the first to put a man in space (Yuri Gagarin, April 1961), first flight of two craft in space (Vostok 3 and 4 in August 1962) and the first woman in space (Valentina Tereshkova, June 1963). Technology as an antidote for societal ills captured the imagination of the Soviet elite – and what could be a better dividend to be paid out to the masses in a country that covered a sixth of the world's landmass than a supersonic airliner?

Supersonic airliner information was among the most sought-after in the cat-and-mouse game of Cold War spying. The Soviets even had a name for their intelligence-gathering efforts against the Anglo-French Concorde: Operation Brunnhilde.

Brunnhilde's greatest coup involved Sergei Fabiew, a high level French technocrat and son of a White Russian, who provided Concorde's entire technical documentation on microfilm to TsAGI, shuttled to the Soviet Union in a hidden compartment behind a heating grill in the first class toilet on the Ostend-Warsaw Express train, and using Aeroflot couriers on scheduled flights.

In Britain, two Kodak workers were tried for espionage at an Old Bailey trial in February 1965, and the same month, Aeroflot's Paris station manager, Sergei Pavlov, was arrested in a Paris restaurant with a napkin containing secrets on landing gear, brakes and high-tech metallurgy. French president Charles de Gaulle was so infuriated that he insisted on personally signing Pavlov's expulsion papers.

Then again – accusations of imitation are an oversimplification. The Soviet Union had a well-developed aviation industry that was in many ways the equal of its western counterpart. Sophisticated technical information obtained through espionage would have been useless if the industrial foundation hadn't existed. And limitations on metallurgy due to the different mineral mix of the Soviet resource base meant some data could only be 'interpreted' rather than copied directly.

Another reason it was impractical to make a direct copy of something found on a stolen blueprint was that the Soviet Union had a very different operating environment to the United States or western Europe, so the hardware had differing operational requirements. And in any case, the Soviets knew they needed a degree of independence because among the wealth of information they had received through espionage,

CCCP-68001 was the first ever Tu-144, serial number zero, seen at the Paris Air Show in June 1971   Jacques Barbé

the French were leaking deliberately doctored data.

Soviet aviation pioneer Andrei Tupolev's son Alexei was by now the chief designer at the Tupolev design bureau, and after discarding over 100 configurations for their proposed supersonic transport, settled on a delta-wing layout, the first aircraft designed in the Soviet Union without a separate horizontal tail surface.

A model of the delta-winged Tu-144 was revealed at the 1965 Paris Air Salon. Technical data described a 120-seater weighing 130 tonnes, able to fly 4,000 miles at Mach 2.3. British intelligence was skeptical about the low weight, and correctly guessed that the engines would need to produce 40,000 lbs of thrust. Tupolev promised a first flight of 1968 – a promise that was kept.

Another model appeared at Expo '67 in Montreal in the flashy $15m Soviet exhibition. The engines were still grouped together at the rear but the intakes split into two pairs.

Three months later, Britain's Minister of Technology Sir John Stonehouse led a British trade mission to the Soviet Union and was able to inspect the prototype Tu-144 in its hangar at Zhukovsky airfield. Stonehouse found the facility primitive, but was impressed by the "unmistakable pterodactyl shape" lurking inside.

Among the delegates to visit was Sir George Edwards, Chairman of the British Aircraft Corporation, who inspected the prototype, after which he told Tupolev the younger, "You've got the intakes and engines in the wrong place. You've got too unsophisticated a wing design, with no camber or twist. Although your bypass engines will help you when it comes to airport noise, you'll lose a lot of efficiency when it comes to your cruise performance." When he added that the engines need to be put "just about halfway across the wing," Tupolev responded, "I know that, but we just can't get the control system to work with an engine out."

In fact both the Tu-144 and Concorde were having trouble with the issue of asymmetrical

CCCP-68001 maiden voyage

The prototype and a pair of production Tu-144s

The cockpit of CCCP-77112　　　　　　　　　　　　　　　　　　　　　　　　　　　**Bahnfrend**

The Tu-144 in flight　　　　　　　　　　　　　　　　　　　　**B. Korzin** Transport-Photo Images

Inflight May 19 1973 — Lev Polikashin RIAN Archive

Main gear cycling — Lev Polikashin RIAN archive

thrust, and much work was already being done by TsAGI to find a way to put the engines out under the wings instead of under the fuselage.

On April 18, 1968, an MiG-21-I, called the *Analog*, got airborne. It had a wing shaped like that of the Tu-144 (hence, "analogous") to give inflight handling experience for designers and pilots alike. The stage was now set for the first flight of the Tu-144.

The final week of 1968 was foggy around Moscow, but December 31 dawned bright, clear and cold. The senior Tupolev, 80 years old the previous week, arrived by limousine to see the 120th (and last) aircraft to bear his name in his lifetime take to the air for its maiden flight, joining workers and onlookers who crowded roofs and balconies.

The Tu-144 prototype, registered CCCP-68001, was pulled from the hangar by a Zil-150 truck, and then to the runway by a Tatra tractor. The pilots arrived, wearing visored helmets, high boots and leather jackets. The captain was Chief Pilot Edward Elyan, 42 years old, born in Baku, who had also been on board the maiden voyage of Tupolev's first jetliner, the Tu-104. His first officer was Mikhail Kozlov, and two flight engineers, V. N. Benderov (who was also head of the entire test programme) and Yuri Seliverstov. The interior of the aircraft was empty, and once inside, the airmen donned pressure suits and strapped into ejector seats.

The deafening thunder of the aircraft's takeoff roll lasted 25 seconds, and the flight that followed, 37 minutes. The landing gear was left down for the whole flight but thousands of parameters were recorded to get the test programme underway.

In the aftermath of the successful first flight, Alexei Tupolev gave a long and frank interview to *Tekhnika Molodezhi* (Technology For Youth) magazine, in which he admitted that supersonic passenger flight was easy. The difficulty was to satisfy the three requirements peculiar to civil aviation – efficiency, reliability, and comfort.

Other publications were more optimistic – *Izvestia* wrote a valentine to the prospect of reaching Khabarovsk, 100 degrees of latitude east of Moscow, in three hours and 20 minutes. A passenger departing Moscow at midday heading west would arrive in Montreal at 9am, thus "outdistancing not only sound but also the sun."

The Tu-144's public debut took place on May 20, 1969 at Moscow's Sheremetyevo airport, and its first supersonic flight took place on June 1, 1970. On July 15, CCCP-68001 hit its record speed for the whole programme of Mach 2.35 (2,443 kmh / 1,517 mph). NATO aptly chose the codename 'Charger'.

The prototype left the Soviet Union for the first time to the 1971 Paris Air Salon from May 25 to June 8, and a programme of demonstration and route-proving flights to Budapest, Hannover and Sofia followed. The Moscow to Sofia leg took place at supersonic speed. One flight involved an emergency landing at the intended destination of Warsaw after two engines failed at the top of descent, probably due to a vibration-induced fatigue crack in the wing, although the aircraft was able to fly home the next day.

The test flights of the prototype had revealed some serious shortcomings. The proximity to the centrally-located engine exhausts produced extreme vibration which even the titanium elements in the fuselage could not withstand. By the time the redesign was complete, not only were upgraded NK-144F engines finally out under the wings in pairs, but also the fuselage had been lengthened (with 34 passenger windows instead of 25) with a new, rounder cross-section, the nose section and radar system altered, and the APU moved from the tail to the starboard engine nacelle.

One of the most notable additions to the production version was the pair of retractable foreplanes, or 'canards'. These were placed just behind the cockpit and were extended at low speed to counter the pitch-down force created by the drooping of the wing's trailing edge 'elevons' which acted as flaps on takeoff and landing.

The production aircraft was designated the Tu-144S and the first example, CCCP-77102, first flew on March 20, 1972 from the factory at Zhukovsky. A month later this aircraft operated a supersonic flight from Moscow to Tashkent in 110 minutes.

Meanwhile, the prototype CCCP-68001's last flight took place on April 27, 1973, at which point she had operated 120 flights, with 180h in the air (including 50h supersonic) and was later broken up, despite her place in history.

CCCP-77102 arrived at Le Bourget airport, Paris, for the 1973 Paris Air Salon after a one hour, 57 minute mostly-supersonic flight from Moscow. On the last day of the airshow, on June 3, she took to the air to perform a display flight under the

CCCP-77110

Guy Viselé

■ ill-fated CCCP-77102 moments before crashing during a display flight at the Paris Air Show — Guy Viselé

command of Captain Mikhail Kozlov, who had been the first officer on the prototype's 1968 maiden flight. Among the other five onboard (first officer, navigator, and three engineers) was V. N. Benderov, another veteran of the maiden flight, and engineer-in-charge of the entire test programme.

The French authorities changed the timings for the Soviet machine's display, reducing the slot to five minutes. After a display by rival Concorde, the Tu-144S got airborne and performed an impressive, if truncated, display. Kozlov brought the big jet down to perform a low pass with gear, flaps and canards extended, then lit the afterburners and climbed steeply away. At 3,000 feet the aircraft was suddenly in trouble. The nose dropped severely and the heavy jetliner was in a rapid descent, close to the ground. A high-G pull up was initiated but it was more than the airframe - any airframe - could take. The left wing folded and the rest of the aircraft rolled inverted, then exploded in front of 300,000 onlookers including most of the world's aviation community.

The village of Goussainville - less than four miles from where Air France 4590 would crash 27 years later - was like a war zone. An engine straddled a garden; a piece of wing fell in the courtyard of the town hall; the cockpit, dead pilots still strapped in, demolished a house; burning fuel ran in the streets and ignited houses and cars. 8 villagers were dead and over 60 seriously injured.

The cause remains hotly debated today. It is generally accepted that a French Mirage fighter jet, probably filming the Soviets' display, came very close to CCCP-77102, surprising its pilots into a violent evasive maneouvre, when they were already disoriented by the shortened slot times that had required them to depart from the routine that had been practiced at least six times over the field back at Zhukovsky.

French TV journalist Michel Tauriac had tried to accompany the flight, but flight engineer Benderov had stopped him, instead taking his camera and promised to film inflight on Tauriac's behalf. A theory widely propounded at the time was that the unsecured camera fouled the first officer's controls, delaying the recovery from the evasive dive.

The crash was a devastating blow but Tupolev and the Soviet aerospace establishment were committed to the programme.

A pair of Tu-144s on the tarmac at Domodedevo frame the men who flew her　　　B. Korzin Transport-Photo Images

Back at the production site in Voronezh, an American delegation arrived, invited prior to the Paris crash, and were impressed by the scale of the project, seeing five aircraft under construction and subassemblies for a dozen more arriving from subcontractors. Mikhail Mikhailov, Deputy Director of the Ministry Of Aviation Production, indicated that Aeroflot had ordered 30 Tu-144s with total orders anticipated of 75.

Foreign visitors meanwhile pondered the "paradox of Voronezh". Outside the factory gates was the real Russia of the time – small villages surrounding a well, linked by dusty unpaved roads past fields where hay was cut with a hand scythe and forked onto a horse drawn cart. It was hard to believe that only a few miles away, a supersonic transport was entering mass production. The concentration of national resources on showcase projects had little effect on the lives of most Soviet citizens.

Routing plans were for "high-priority industrial traffic" from Moscow to Novosibirsk, Irkutsk and Khabarovsk in 1975. A second tranche of five routes were planned – to those three cities from Leningrad (now St Petersburg), plus Moscow to Tashkent and to Alma Ata (now Almaty). Later routes would include the United States, Singapore and Tokyo.

■ Ramp ceremony at Alma Ata moments after the arrival of the Tu-144 on its first revenue passenger flight, November 1 1977
B. Korzin Transport-Photo Images

■ After refuelling, part two of the Tu-144's first revenue flight as it prepares to set sail on the return leg to Moscow
B. Korzin Transport-Photo Images

■ Interestingly, unlike the its Western supersonic rival, the British-French Concorde, the Tu-144 had two class passenger accomodation, with 2-1 seating in first class and 3-2 in economy
Pavel Vanka

■ Economy class; both of these images were taken aboard CCCP-77106
Simon De Rudder

■ CCCP-77115 was the last Tu-144D to fly, taking to the skies on October 4, 1984; later donated to the club Heroes Of The Soviet Union for preservation at Zhukovsky
Guy Viselé

■ The last Tu-144 post retirement at Zhukovsky

Fyodor Borisov Transport-Photo Images

In fact the Tu-144 was far from entering service. Aeroflot's enthusiasm for the type cooled off over the next couple of years, with no announcements of an entry into service. The test programme continued to struggle with thirsty NK-144F engines and a lack of the refinement required for passenger comfort.

Freight and mail service from Moscow Domodedovo to Alma Ata (now Almaty) in Soviet Kazakhstan began on December 26, 1975 with CCCP-77106. These non-passenger flights were also used to check the new type's compatibility with ground handling equipment and its ability to fit among subsonic traffic at commercial airports during takeoff and landing, although the payload was incidental – these were still test flights in all but name, and ended in December 1976.

The first passenger service, flight SU 499, finally took place November 1, 1977, from Moscow's Domodedovo airport to Alma Ata, operated by CCCP-77109, a new-build Tu-144S. At Domodedovo, assembled dignitaries included Alexei Tupolev, Minister of Aircraft Industry Pyotr Dementyev, and Minister of Civil Aviation Boris Bogayev. Speeches were made linking the new supersonic airliner to the 60th anniversary of the Russian revolution, and passengers boarded after a delay due to a broken set of boarding stairs. Captain Boris Kuznetsov took CCCP-77109 into the air operating SU499 at 0903 local time and landed at Alma Ata at 1102. The return flight, SU 500, took off at 1328 and landed back in Moscow at 1531.

This was the first time non-Soviet passengers were carried, and reports were mixed. While window shades dropping of their own accord and an inoperative toilet can be dismissed as growing pains, there was a major problem. While Concorde used an intricate system of pipes to pump fuel under the skin to absorb the heat of high-speed flight-induced friction, the Tupolev used massive air-conditioning packs. The ear-shattering roar made normal conversation impossible, and passengers had to communicate by passing handwritten notes. If anything, it was even worse in the back rows, closest to the bellowing engines.

Although the next two flights after the inaugural service were cancelled, SU 499 operated weekly on Tuesdays leaving Moscow at 0830 and SU 500 leaving Alma Ata for the return flight to the capital at 1530. The fare was 68 Rubles instead of the subsonic fare of 48 Rubles. Foreign nationals were onboard virtually every flight; even with the cost of acquiring a visa and travelling to the Soviet Union, this was still a much cheaper option than a Concorde ticket for those who wanted to break the sound barrier.

On April 27, 1978, the first production airframe of the final variant, the Tu-144D (D for long range) flew for the first time, powered by the long-awaited Kolesov RD-36-51 turbojet engines, which finally enabled the intended supercruise speed of Mach 2.

The Tu-144D variant, however, was fated to never see passenger service. Disaster struck on May 23, 1978 during a routine test flight near Moscow, when CCCP-77111, a brand-new Tu-144D, suffered a crack in a fuel line in the starboard wing during her sixth flight. When the APU was started, the leaking fuel ignited a massive fire. The pilots, B. Popov and Edward Yelian, managed a reasonably effective wheels-up landing in a field near Yegoryevsk, but the two engineers who had been sent back to the passenger cabin for safety were both killed when the deflected nose cone dug into the ground, broke away and punctured the fuselage exactly where they were sitting.

Passenger flights were suspended – the last SU 499/500 roundtrip operated on June 1, 1978. Production and testing continued. However on July 31, CCCP-77113 suffered a compressor disc failure during supersonic flight, causing structural and systems damage. The crew were able to decelerate and land safely on the 11,500 ft runway at Engels-2 bomber base near Saratov, streaming smoke with instrument panels lit up like Christmas trees.

Freight flights resumed on June 23, 1979, from Moscow to Khabarovsk in far eastern Russia, showing that the Tu-144D's Kolesov RD-36-51 engines had finally allowed the programme to ovecome the range issues of the earlier turbofan-powered Tu-144S, but it was too little too late. In the final reckoning, a total of only 102 revenue flights ever operated, including 55 passenger flights that carried only 3,284 passengers.

The Tu-144 had enough supporters to continue test flights, and on February 20, 1981, was reissued with a Provisional Flight Certificate, but never returned to passenger flights. On July 1, 1983, government order 461-169 ended production of the aircraft and stated that the future of the type should only be for research flights. Within weeks, CCCP-77114, a brand-new Tu-144D, set thirteen world records for speed and altitude, recognised by the Fédération Aéronautique Internationale (FAI), the world's governing body for aeronautical world records, and between 1986 and 1989 this airframe was used for medical research into high-altitude radiological effects. Another Tu-144D was used during 1985 to train cosmonauts for missions on the Buran space shuttle.

In the early 1990s, a study group consisting of Tupolev, NASA, Rockwell and Boeing was co-ordinated by Judith DePaul of IBP Aerospace, to examine the prospects of a future supersonic airliner, known as SST-2. For a flying testbed, Russian authorities reactivated CCCP-77114, a low-time airframe, even after its record breaking and research flights of the 1980s. CCCP-77112 was used as a ground test rig and CCCP-77115 was on standby as a 'hot reserve'.

Some US voices questioned the wisdom of using a Russian airframe with most of the $35m budget being spent inside Russia - the Cold War having ended only a few years earlier. Louis Williams, head of NASA's High Speed Research Program, explained in several interviews why the Tu-144 was uniquely suited to the role - the supersonic research platform should come as close as possible to a future SST-2 in performance (Mach 2.3 instead of Concorde's Mach 2) and size (wing area of 507m sq instead of Concorde's 425 m sq). Also helpful was that the Tu-144 had the biggest share of titanium in its empty weight - 20% - compared to any other aircraft.

Conversion included refitting the aircraft with new engines, Kuzhnetsov NK-321 afterburning turbofans, similar to the powerplants fitted to the Tupolev Tu-160 Blackjack supersonic bomber. Reregistered RA-77114 and painted in an all-white livery and US and Russian flags together on the tail (and titles in Boeing's Stratotype font), the Tu-144LL (LL for flying laboratory), the reactivated airliner took to the air on November 29, 1996 and performed a total of 27 test flights, with the final sortie on February 28, 1998, gathering important data about high speed, high altitude flight by large aircraft.

RA-77114 made one last flight, which was also the last flight of a Tupolev Tu-144 anywhere: a test flight and last waltz from its home base of Zhukovsky, on April 14, 1999.

The story of the Tu-144 bears much similarity to that of the Concorde - conceived in an era when the promise of technology was limitless, yet sunk by the cost of energy and the competing appeal of capacity over speed. The Tu-144 was undone by the economics of the widebody Ilyushin Il-86 just as surely as Concorde was by the Boeing 747.

The Tu-144's 55 passenger flights were a bone-shaking, white-knuckle shriek to the edge of space and back; uncomfortable and even frightening perhaps, but at speeds more than double those of today's passenger liners. Despite the marginal technology used, those flights all made it to their destination in Kazakhstan safely, and back. In addition to this important standard, there is no doubt that building and flying a supersonic airliner constitutes one of the ambitious of all our efforts to conquer the skies, and there may never be another. This one is certainly worth remembering.

■ **Tupolev Tu-144: production list**
CCCP registration and current status (total airframe hours)
77101 to 77106 test aircraft only
77106 to 77115 delivered to Aeroflot

■ **Prototype Tu-144**
68001 broken up unknown year (180h)

■ **Pre-production Tu-144S**
77101 broken up 1978 (339h)

■ **Production Tu-144S**
77102 crashed Goussainville 3/6/73 (approx. 200h)
77103 broken up 1984 (313h)
77104 (reregistered 77144) broken up, 1987 (431h)
77105 broken up 1995 (314h)
77106 display Soviet Air Force Museum, Monino, Moscow (582h 36m)
77107 ground instructional airframe, State Technical University, Kazan (357h)
77108 ground instructional airframe, State Technical University, Samara (68h)
77109 stored Voronezh (unknown hours)
77110 display Civil Air Fleet Museum, Ulyanovsk (314h)

■ **Production Tu-144D**
77111 crashed Yegoryevsk 23/5/78 (9h 2m)
77112 display Auto and Technik Museum, Sinsheim (197h 45m)
77113 broken up 2001 (223h)
77114 (Tu-144LL testbed) stored, Zhukovsky (443h 28m)
77115 stored Zhukovsky (38h 34m)
77116 not completed / stored, Zhukovsky (-)

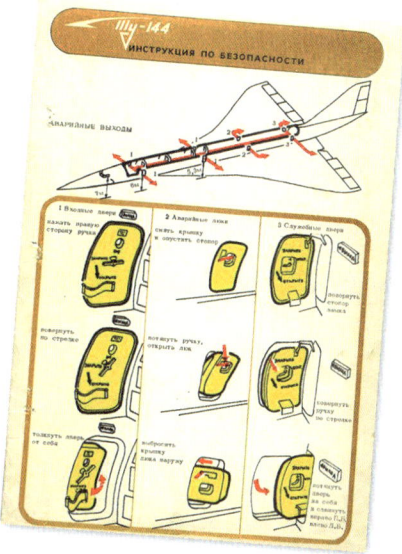

■ The Tu-144 catches up with its photoship chase plane   **B. Korzin** Transport-Photo Images

Fyodor Borisov Transport-Photo Images

Tupolev Tu-154
The workhorse

Tu-154 is in many ways the definitive Soviet airliner – a true workhorse with nearly one thousand built.

The Tu-154 design represented an important step forward for the Tupolev OKB. The Tu-104 and Tu-124 were both direct relations of the Tu-16 jet bomber, and the Tu-134 was a direct descendant of the Tu-104; the Tu-114 turboprop was closely based on the Tu-95 *Bear*. The Tu-154, on the other hand, was the first jetliner that started with a completely clean sheet and other than aeronautics and aerofoil design expertise, owed nothing to a previous type.

One of the main aims of the new machine was to replace the Antonov An-10, the Ilyushin Il-18 and the Tupolev Tu-104. All had advantages inherent in their design – the An-10 had excellent short and rough field performance, the Il-18 had unrivalled fuel efficiency, and the Tu-104 was fast. But three very different types from three different design bureaux created logistical headaches for maintenance, spares availability, and the inability to be moved around Aeroflot's vast route network interchangeably.

Therefore the bar was high – the new design had to incorporate the best of all its predecessors, if not exceed them. An early design known as the Tu-104D had a three-engine configuration that was prescient, and in 1963 this layout was dusted off and expanded upon, although other arrangements were considered, such as a straight-through duct for number two engine (like the DC-10) or four engines in pairs either side of the rear fuselage (like the Il-62 or Lockheed Jetstar). A 3.8 metre (12.47 feet) fuselage diameter was chosen, with accommodation in two classes for 109 passengers, or for 141 in a high density all-economy layout.

By mid-1965 the design was frozen around three Kuznetsov NK-8 turbofans with number two engine fed by an S-duct intake above the rear fuselage in the style of the era, as seen on the Hawker Siddeley Trident and Boeing 727. On August 24, 1965 the Soviet Council of Ministers issued directive no. 647-240, instructing the Tupolev OKB to build the new plane (after rejecting a similar design from the Ilyushin OKB which would have been known as the Il-72).

The design was chosen as it incorporated state-of-the-art technology which made it particularly versatile. The large wing (180 square metres compared to 145 on the Boeing 727) made it possible to reach high cruising altitudes, up to 12,000 metres (39,370 feet) with very low fuel consumption, as well as reducing the approach speed to as slow as 180 kph (100 knots). A high thrust-to-weight ratio gave excellent airfield performance with an ability to operate from runways as short as 1,500 metres (4,921 feet) and from 'hot and high' fields in which atmospheric conditions reduced lift and thrust.

The very first Tu-154, prototype CCCP-85000, Le Bourget June 6, 1969 — Jacques Barbé

Flexibility was built into the passenger accommodation – seat tracks on the floor enabled quick changes to seating density as the three-seat units on either side of the aisle (for a total of six abreast) could be moved closer or further apart, depending on the mission. The last row could be replaced by a bolt-in closet for winter coats.

Work on the prototype took place through most of 1968 at the MMZ Opyt near Moscow. After completion and static testing on the systems, it was disassembled and trucked to the flight test facility at Zhukovsky, registered CCCP-85000, and prepared for its first flight.

Captain Yu. V. Sukhov took the impressive new machine into the air for the first time on October 3, 1968. With him on the flight deck was co-pilot N. N. Kharitonov and flight engineer V. I. Yevdokimov. In the main cabin, filled with test and measuring equipment, were test engineers L. A. Yumashev, Yu. G. Yefimov, and electronics specialist Yu. G. Kumenko.

After 12 flights, and some modifications that resulted from the data acquired along the way, the test programme was integrated with the authorities of the State Civil Aviation Research Institute. The Soviet Union drafted common airworthiness regulations in the mid-sixties and published their regulations as NLGS-1 in 1967; the Tu-154 was the first airliner to be developed and certified using this code. Test flying lasted from December 1968 until January 1971. The certification phase then ran from June to December 1971.

In early 1969 test flying was interrupted to prepare for the type's international debut at the 27th Paris Air Show, which required the creation of a typical airliner cabin. Trim, carpet, seating and overhead racks were installed and on May 25, CCCP-85000's 43rd flight was to Le Bourget where the world's aviation community was gathered. The cabin and cockpit was open for inspection to all, and the reaction was generally favourable despite a few chauvinistic sneers ('...a general inattention to aerodynamic detail' claimed one uncomprehending critic). For the benefit of the press in Aeroflot's home market, a promotional flight was operated from Moscow's Vnukovo airport to nearby Sheremeteyevo on August 12.

Factory No. 18 in Kuibyshev was chosen for mass production of the Tu-154. The city of one million people, renamed Samara in 1991, situated on the Volga river, is a centre of aerospace excellence, where Factory No. 18 pumped out over 900 Tupolev Tu-154s as part of a technology cluster surrounding the city's industrial Bezymyanka airport, which also included State Aviation Plant No. 1 which traced its history back to workshops established in Moscow in 1917 to make bicycles, motorcycles, and small aeroplanes, and moved to Kuibyshev in 1941 to build Ilyushin Il-2 and Il-10 warplanes. After the war, State Aviation Plant No. 1 was building MiG-15 fighter jets, and by the end of the 1950s had changed its name to Progress Rocket Space Centre and was in the spaceflight business. Indeed, Yuri Gagarin went to Kuibyshev to rest after his first – the first – trip into space, and his first public words were with an improvised meeting of Progress workers. Only southern California, with Lockheed, McDonnell Douglas, Honeywell, General Dynamics, Northrop-Grumman et al had an aerospace establishment as formidable.

The first preproduction Tu-154s rolled out in late 1969 to join the test programme, registered CCCP-85001, 85002, 85003 and 85004. 001 and 002 were used to explore handling at high angles of attack, and stall and spin tests, prioritised after a number of crashes in the early days of the Tu-104. 002 was fitted with a spin recovery parachute

Tu-154 flyby — Lev Polikashin

in place of the APU (auxiliary power unit) which meant it had to rely on ground power for engine start. It was also fitted with an escape hatch for bailing out in flight, in case spin recovery was impossible.

As the test programme went on, the flap control system was modified, engines were tweaked, ease of access for maintenance was found to be lacking in some areas and hence improved where possible, and the cabin layout needed a few changes, but the test programme showed that the Tu-154 basically met or exceeded expectations.

CCCP-85012 was a very early build Tu-154, introduced into service in 1971 and retired in April 1994 — **Guy Viselé**

1980s Tu-154 action at Tyumen; CCCP-85522 later became part of the Tyumen Airlines fleet
Valentin Grebnev Transport-Photo Images

The first six preproduction machines were delivered to the Moscow Vnukovo CAD in late 1970 for evaluation and to begin crew training. Route proving trips carrying cargo and mail began in May 1971 to Tbilisi, Simferopol, Sochi, and Mineralnye Vody. On February 5, 1972, civil aviation minister Boris P. Bugayev signed an order clearing the Tu-154 for passenger service.

The first revenue passenger flight took place on February 9 (Aeroflot's 49th birthday) from Moscow Vnukovo to Mineralnye Vody, operated by CCCP-85016 and operated by captain Ye. I. Bagmut. At the press conference before the flight, test pilot Grigoriy A. Nikiforov told the media, "The Tu-154 is a subsonic aircraft but it really makes you feel like you could go supersonic, so great are its power reserves and so refined are its aerodynamics." The first revenue international flight by Tu-154 was operated by CCCP-85201 from Moscow to Berlin Schönefeld on April 2, 1972, followed by Prague on August 1.

Production at Kuibyshev began ramping up, with 12 machines manufactured in 1971, 12 in 1972, 18 in 1973, 37 in 1974 and 42 in 1975 – from one a month to almost one a week. As with the Tu-134, the first export customer was Balkan Bulgarian Airlines, with LZ-BTA and BTB delivered to Sofia in May 1972, followed by BTC in March 1973. Malev Hungarian Airlines was the second export customer, receiving three Tu-154 *sans suffixe* machines starting with HA-LCA which inaugurated service to Moscow on September 13, 1973

Pilots both domestic and international were trained at the Ulyanovsk Higher Civil Aviation Flying School, part of the COMECON Civil Aviation Centre. It was only after several years of Tu-154 operations that the first simulator, known as the KTS-Tu-154, arrived on the scene; until that point all training was done on the real thing, and continued under the supervision of training captains when trainees returned to their bases at the end of their typerating course.

The roll-out of the Tu-154 onto Aeroflot's route map showed the new Soviet flagship was as versatile as had been hoped. It demonstrated its people-moving capabilities on the short but heavily trafficked Moscow to Leningrad run, and stretched its legs flying from Moscow to Mirny, which at 5,230 kilometres (3,248 miles) is the exact same distance as London to Montreal. The Leningrad base used their new Tu-154s to replace the Tu-104 on international routes to Stockholm and Oslo, while the Central Directorate of International Flights opened up Moscow to Marseilles, Milan, and to

1981-build in Dushanbe where it remained after the break up of the Soviet Union flying with Tajik Air until retirement in 2007
Valentin Grebnev Transport-Photo Images

Aden via Athens and Cairo. The Far Eastern CAD began flying from Khabarovsk to Niigata in Japan and Pyongyang in North Korea.

After the production of 42 Tu-154 *sans suffixe* machines, Kuznetsov had created an uprated NK-8 engine was ready to be incorporated into the new Tu-154A version, of which 50 were built; the extra thrust required a visually distinctive ring of 12 blow-in doors around the leading edge of the engine nacelle to improve the engines' surge performance. The additional thrust increased the maximum takeoff weight by two tonnes to 94 tonnes and the payload weight by the same amount to 18 tonnes. An extra fuel tank was added to the wing box which helped with stability in flight and allowed extra range – or tankering of fuel for return trips back from remote destinations which lacked facilities. Other modifications included simplified flap and slat controls (although these were prone to mechanical shortcomings in flight for some time after), new shock absorbers on the main gear (curing the *sans suffixe* trait of bouncing on landing) and a fatter bullet fairing at the leading edge of the top of the vertical fin, housing the new *Mikron* HF radio antenna.

At the time it was adopted for use in the wing structure, the properties of V95 aluminium had not been studied fully, and while its flexibility was welcomed by passengers and crew because it was very effective at smoothing out the ride en route, its fatigue resistance turned out to be inadequate, and cracks were appearing in the wings of even the newest machines. Tupolev had no choice but to create a new wing structure of stiffer D16 duralumin, with complete wing sets retrofitted to all existing machines as well as new-builds.

Two important changes were made to the control surfaces: the ailerons were shortened, now ending two metres (six feet six inches) short of the wing tips, and the span of the spoilers was widened to match that of the trailing edge flaps. This was done to move roll forces closer to the centreline of the aircraft, reducing wing flex. With the new wings fitted, a Tu-154A became a Tu-154B, and soon there were no Tu-154As left in service. The first designated Tu-154B entered service domestically October 1, 1975, followed by a first international trip from Leningrad to London on December 30.

The Tu-154B-1 was a subvariant that had some minor interior layout changes and one extra passenger window; 64 B-1s were built, starting with CCCP-85231 on September 1, 1977. The Tu-154B-2

CCCP-85012, the 12th Tu-154, scrapped at Irkutsk in April 1994, seen here at Le Bourget May 31, 1973   Jacques Barbé

followed with CCCP-85295 in September 1978, and this became the dominant version of the Tu-154B with 311 rolling off the line at Kuibyshev, including Salon VIP machines.

Three Tu-154Bs were leased by Malev from Aeroflot in 1975 while their original trio had new wings fitted. One of the leased Aeroflot machines crashed on September 9, 1975 into Lebanese territorial waters while landing in war-torn Beirut in an accident that remains controversial to this day – officialdom will not be drawn on the findings of the investigation "for reasons not connected to the crash" and questions put to the European Union as recently as January 2009 have gone unanswered; a shootdown is suspected, due to presence of persons or payload on the flight relating to the Lebanese civil war. Nine Tu-154B-2s joined Malev in the late seventies and stayed up to the turn of the century, some being converted to small package freighters with main deck payload being loaded through passenger doors.

Romania was a keen adopter of new aviation technology as evidenced by its ability to construct BAC-111s under licence from the British Aircraft Corporation, and its airline TAROM received the first of 12 Tu-154Bs in June 1976, operated in a two-class configuration of ten first class and 135 economy seats, or a 164 all-economy configuration. One aircraft was operated as a head-of-state VIP aircraft (YR-TPJ).

Even as the Tu-154B variants began taking to the skies, plans were made for a radical overhaul to the Tu-154 design, starting with the application of the Solviev D-30 engines that had been designed for the Ilyushin Il-62M, which had a much higher bypass ratio than the existing NK-8 powerplant (2.43 instead of 1.05) and other enhancements such as clamshell reverse thrust system instead of the old-fashioned cascade type.

This set off a series of other changes, including a completely new fuselage aft of the rear pressure bulkhead to accommodate the larger D-30 in the number two engine position, and engine numbers one and three were repositioned higher on the side of the fuselage to lift the thrust line. The wing-fuselage join was streamlined, which necessitated a tweak to the shape of the trailing edge flaps, which were also sealed to create less drag when retracted. New leading edge slats

LZ-BTM served Balkan Bulgarian for its whole life, from delivery in May 1977 until scrapping in Sofia in 1996, seen here landing at London Heathrow in April 1982
Richard Vandervord

spanned the entire wing without a break. The area of the horizontal stabiliser was increased. The APU was moved from its original position at the base of the rudder to a bay beneath the S-duct of number two engine. In keeping with established Soviet practice for the second generation of an aircraft type, the new variant was designated the Tu-154M.

The first Tu-154M prototype was converted from an extant Tu-154B-2, CCCP-85317, and made its first flight with all the modifications both external and internal from Kuibyshev in early 1980, with Tupolev test pilot Sergei T. Agapov in the left seat. State acceptance trials took place between June 1 and August 14, 1981.

Around the same time, it was decided by the authorities and Aeroflot that 200 low-time Tu-154B-2s should be converted to Tu-154M standard at the end of the 1980s, and a conversion kit was created. Soon after, however, the plan changed back, as it was ascertained that the available resources would be better deployed building more new Tu-154Ms and letting the Tu154Bs fly on unchanged. Indeed the oldest government and military Tu-154 *sans suffixe* and B models were flown with a reduced cabin pressure to extend the structural life of those machines.

Four years after the first proof-of-concept Tu-154M flight with CCCP-85317, the first true Tu-154M, effectively the second prototype, finally took to the air. Registered CCCP-85606, the flight took place on July 16, 1984, flown by a Tupolev crew led by A. I. Talalakin. Three more aircraft were produced the same year, mostly for the test programme, and full-scale production began in January 1985.

Aeroflot's base at Moscow's Vnukovo airport was the first to receive the newest Tupolev, and Balkan Bulgarian Airlines was once again the first international carrier to take delivery of a Tu-154M. The acceptance into service was without incident, and the increased efficiency and reduced fuel burn was welcome (the M burned up to 1,000 kilograms less fuel per hour than the B). The only backwards step was the D-30 engines were smokier than the NK-8s. Later, in the nineties when Tu-154Ms ended up in the hands of dozens of Babyflots after the break up of the Soviet Union, many airline liveries used darker colours to mask the soot that would build up around the rear fuselage due to the efflux of reverse thrust.

■ RA-85595 was one of the last Tu-154B-2s built, delivered to Aeroflot on January 31, 1984, and flew on with Orenair and UTAir
Dubai **Chris Doggett**

■ RA-85508 taxis out at Yekaterinburg ahead of other Ural Airlines Tu-154s, August 1999 **Richard Vandervord**

■ RA-85687 was delivered to Aeroflot in December 1990 and went on to S7 and later Iran Air Tours, and was scrapped at Mineralniye Vody in 2013 Novosibirsk July 2005 **Richard Vandervord**

Balkan operated a total of 25 owned airframes and an additional 22 on lease; although the airline acquired Boeing 737s and 767s in the 1990s, the Tu-154s remained on strength flying charter flights up until the sale of the airline to Israeli finance company Ze'evi, under whose stewardship the airline went bankrupt.

The Tu-154M found a couple of other operators in Europe that had thus far resisted the charms of the earlier variants. Poland's long-established carrier LOT relied on the Tu-134 and Il-18 for shorthaul flying while its Il-62s were maxed out flying transatlantic to New York, Chicago and Toronto. In the mid-eighties it needed extra capacity and leased three Tu-154B-2s from Aeroflot's Leningrad base starting in May 1985, followed by 14 owned Tu-154Ms, starting with SP-LCA on May 27, 1986. However, even before the final delivery, of SP-LCO in January 1991, LOT began acquiring western hardware, starting with Boeing 767-200s and -300s and followed by 737s; the last Tu-154 flight was on August 15, 1994, with most of the fleet sold to Russian airlines.

SP-LCO remained in Poland and was reregistered 862 Black, later simply 102, to form half of the head of state transport fleet alongside 837 Black, later 101, a new-build Salon machine. 101 made headlines worldwide when it crashed in thick fog near Smolensk on the morning of April 10, 2010 after descending below decision height without visual contact with the ground. All 96 on board, who made up virtually all of the country's apparatus of governance, were killed: the president and first lady, military top brass including the chiefs of staff of all three branches (air force, army, navy), the president of the National Bank, 18 members of parliament, the head of the Olympic Committee, the head of the National Security Bureau (equivalent to the FBI or MI5), senior members of the clergy. The highest death toll in a Tu-154 crash was Aeroflot 7425, a Tu-154B-2 lost in Uzbekistan on July 10, 1985 after a high altitude stall resulted in an unrecoverable flat spin that killed all 191 passengers

■ Postcard of a locally-based Tu-154B at Yerevan in Soviet Armenia

■ Tu-154 line up   **Guy Viselé**

and nine crew; but the loss of the Polish Air Force 101 was the most devastating for a country and in some circles to this day the most controversial.

Czechoslovakia's flag carrier CSA was another latecomer to the "Studio 154" party, receiving the first of seven, a Tu-154M, at the beginning of 1988, inaugurating service to London Heathrow on March 5 as OK754/755. As the 1990s progressed, the type was supplanted on scheduled service by new Boeing 737s, and was mostly used for its people-carrying capabilities on flights to beaches, operating its last flight for the airline on a charter flight from Istanbul to Prague on January 10, 2000. The government also operated four Tu-154B-2s and three Tu-154Ms.

Tu-154B 552 was delivered to North Korea in 1976 seen in Stockholm May 24, 1976 — **Jacques Barbé**

552 still flies with the DPRK flag carrier today, sporting Air Koryo's new livery in Vladivostok, August 2016 — **Oleg Ivanchenko**

Interestingly, East Germany's airline Interflug never operated the Tu-154, with the Tu-134 covering most local flying within Europe and the mighty Ilyushin Il-62, usually tasked with long haul flights, stepping in to provide extra shorthaul capacity when needed. The government of the German Democratic Republic did operate two Tu-154M Salon VIP aircraft, which were taken over by the unified Luftwaffe after the fall of the Berlin Wall; one was lost in a freakish midair collision with a USAF Lockheed C-141B Starlifter in the vast empty skies of the South Atlantic Ocean on September 13, 1997.

The Tu-154 was an export success further afield. For North Korea's flag carrier Air Koryo (then known as Choson Minhang), four Tu-154As (later converted to B standard with new wings and engines) were its first jet equipment, replacing the Il-18 on the long trip to Moscow (the Hawker Siddeley Trident was also considered). Two Tu-154s remain airworthy today as part of the airline's heritage fleet, operating short flights within the country and charter flights for groups of aviation enthusiasts. South Yemen's carrier Alyemda bought its first Tu-154 in 1981 and added a second in 1989, flying them locally and to Europe until 1992. Bakhtar Afghan Airlines (later returning to its previous name Ariana Afghan) bought two machines new from the factory in 1987.

Chinese operators collectively ordered 36, operated by CAAC, Air Great Wall, China Northwest Airlines, China Southwest Airlines, China Xinjiang Airlines, Sichuan Airlines and the People's Liberation Army Air Force's airline, China United Airlines. Cubana operated nine out of their tropical base at Havana. Neighbouring Guyana Airlines initialled leased a handful of Tu-154B-2s from TAROM and later bought a Tu-154M directly. Pakistan's flag carrier PIA leased three aircraft starting in 1996 from an Uzbek owner for flights to Saudi Arabia, and seven were leased to Pakistani independent carrier Shaheen Air International between 1999 and 2005, four from Belarus and three from Russia's Bashkirian Airlines. Three Tu-154s had a flying career in Turkey, first of all with leisure carrier Greenair between 1990 and 1993 and later with Active Air in 1995.

Egyptair ordered eight Tu-154As with the first delivery taking place in December 1973; however, head of Egypt's CAA Gamal Erfun was vocally critical of what he perceived to be design flaws, and the Tu-154 was calculated to be more expensive per hour for the airline to operate than their fleet of Boeing 707s. Before a final decision could be made about the type's future with the airline, SU-AXO crashed on a training flight near Cairo airport on July 10, 1974, killing six pilots and ending the type's short career in Egypt. Syrianair had a more positive experience with the type, running three of Tu-154Ms out of Damascus between 1985 and 1998, mostly to Moscow, Athens and the Persian Gulf (interestingly, alongside three Boeing 727s). Air Somalia operated a Tu-154B-2 out of Sharjah to the wartorn city of Mogadishu in 2001.

In the Middle East, by far the biggest operator of the Tu-154 was Iran, who, due to a political falling out with erstwhile ally the United States in the wake of the Iranian Revolution of 1979, found itself unable to add to what was up to that point a large and growing fleet of Boeings including seven 747s. As the population and the economy of Iran grew, especially once the defensive war against Saddam Hussein's Iraq which at that time backed by the West, was won in 1988, the capacity gap in Iran's airline network was filled by a cosmopolitan selection of Tu-154s. In the early years of the twenty-first century, the Tu-154 became as common on the ramp at Tehran's downtown Mehrabad as it was in Moscow.

Aircraft were provided to Iran with flight deck crew (cabin crew were locals) and in most cases the ships were not fully painted in the local airline's colours, retaining cheatlines and base liveries that made their provenance obvious. Aria Air, Caspian Airlines, Kish Air, Eram Air, Zagros Airlines, Taban Air, Mahan Air, and Qeshm Airlines

▰ After three years with Aeroflot and a decade with Rossiya, EY-85651, seen here landing in Dubai, went to Aviacon Zitotrans and Tajik Air before ending up at Taban Air in Iran **Guy Viselé**

▰ Delivered to CAAC in April 1986, this bird flew for China Northwest, Donbass in Ukraine, and Qeshm Air of Iran; it went on to fly for six years at Donavia and was scrapped at Rostov-on-Don **Bruno Geiger**

▰ Caspian Airlines' ill-fated EP-CPG at Tehran Imam Khomeini on May 21, 2009, 56 days before it crashed on the way to Yerevan with the loss of all 168 onboard **Guy Van Herbruggen**

were among the Persian operators of the Tu-154, however the most prolific operator was Iran Air subsidiary Iran Air Tours, with a total of 81 Tu-154s passing through the airline's ranks.

Unfortunately the Tu-154 had a rather accident-prone career in Iran, with serious crashes befalling Iran Air Tours with 278 dead in three separate fatal disasters, a runway accident with Taban Air in Mashhad, and Caspian Airlines 7908, whose death toll of 168 was the second-worst air disaster of 2009 (second only to Air France 447) and came only days after the fatal crash of an Il-62 in Mashhad operating on behalf of Aria Air. This led to the Iranian travelling public becoming fearful of "Tupolev" planes (and Iran Air Tours in particular), and for once statistics were on the side of nervous passengers, as ten percent of all Tu-154 accidents took place in Iran. Accusations that Russian airlines took the opportunity to send their least reliable planes and least skilled pilots were probably without foundation but there is no doubt that the task of certifying and monitoring the operation was a monumental challenge to the Iranian authorities, as the flight deck crew and mechanics that accompanied the planes only spoke Russian, as was the case with flight deck instrumentation and aircraft manuals. After this chequered Persian career, but having filled a vital capacity gap in a huge and populous country, the Tu-154 was banned from Iranian airlines on February 19, 2011. A long-overdue treaty covering Iran's nuclear technology was agreed with seven world powers which would have enabled Iranian airlines to order large numbers of brand-new hardware direct from the manufacturer for the first time since the seventies but this is now in doubt after the treaty was violated by the United States under President Donald Trump.

One Tu-154 with a taste for mystery turned up in Rwanda (as 9XR-DU) and Central African Republic (TL-ACF). Guyana Airways operated three on lease from TAROM, and one registered in Guyana as 8R-GGA. The Ethiopian Air Force operated one with the military serial 1061, withdrawn from use at the remote airfield of Debre Zeyit.

As the Soviet Union crumbled at the end of the 1980s, Kuibyshev was renamed Samara, and Factory No. 18 was privatised and changed its name to AVIS Joint Stock Company, later Aviacor. Production of the Tu-154M continued apace for the first half of the 1990s. The twin-engined Tu-204 was intended to replace the Tu-154, and although the Tu-204 did go into production (indeed, at two different sites – the Aviastar plant at Ulyanovsk and KAPO in Kazan), actual numbers were vanishingly small, exceeding five airframes a year only in 1993 (five), 2008 (ten), 2009 (six) and 2011 (five) for a total of 63 Tu-204s in 28 years (15 different years saw only one or two airframes completed).

Because commitments to build Tu-154s were in place and it was easier to follow through and build those planes than to switch to the more expensive and high tech Tu-204, so 1990, 1991, 1992 and 1993 all saw nearly 40 airframes a year roll off the line. Only in 1994 did production slow, initally to seven for the year, and then a handful after that; 1998 was the final year of consistent production with five built. The last production machines were delivered with modern avionics including Flight Management System computers (FMS), a Ground Proximity Warning System (GPWS) and Traffic Collision Avoidance System (TCAS), plus cabin tweaks including bigger overhead bins. These were dubbed the Tu-154M-100 and three were delivered to Slovak Airlines in 1998 and later sold on to

■ Taban Air flight 6437 ended in a non-fatal crash at Mashhad, but signalled the end of Tu-154 operations in Iran   **IRNA**

Russian airlines in 2003. After that, an occasional Tu-154M was built using leftover hulls and wing sets up until 2005, followed by a final machine delivered to the Russian Ministry of Defence on February 19, 2013.

Over 40 Tu-154s were delivered to the air force of the Soviet Union, and in the post-Soviet period operated by various arms of the Russian military including the Air Force, the Ministry of the Interior, the Naval Air Arm, and the Russia State Transport Co (later rebranded as Rossiya Airlines as some of its operations were commercial).

Production of the Tu-154 can be divided into two similarly-sized chunks; the first being *sans suffixe*, A, B and B-2 models, and the second being the M models. However there were a number of other variants produced, such as the Tu-154S, a convertible freighter with a main cargo door on the left side of the fuselage; nine aircraft were thus modified and placed into service, mostly operating out of Aeroflot bases in Khabarovsk and Dushanbe.

The Tu-154 played an important role in the Soviet space programme. The Soviet project to build a reusable space transport vehicle, became the Buran ("Snowstorm") spaceship which began in earnest in the late 1970s. Unlike the Shuttle, Buran was intended to have fully automatic landing capability, and three Tu-154Bs were converted to flying avionics testbeds and cosmonaut trainers with a Buran pilot's workstation replacing the first officer's instruments and controls, plus a complete Buran cockpit in the forward passenger cabin; these machines were known as the Tu-154LL (for Flying Laboratory). To replicate the brick-like flying characteristics of the orbiter, reverse thrust and full ground spoilers were used in flight. Nearly 300 flights were performed, testing 16 different automatic landing systems. Buran successfully made its own fully-automatic space launch and return on November 15, 1988. Other Tu-154LLs were used to test laminar flow and dubbed the Tu-154LL-ULO, and a total inflight simulator (TIFS) testbed for new control systems including digital fly-by-wire and head-up displays was the Tu-154LL-FACT.

The most radical variant was the Tu-155 cyrogenic fuel demonstrator. Steep rises in the price of energy in the 1970s meant research into alternative fuels became a high priority. Natural gas exists in far greater abundance than crude oil, especially within the territory of the Soviet Union,

■ S7 Tu-154M back in the Aviacor factory in Samara where it was originally built, for a heavy check   Aviacor

A line up of Sibir aka S7 Tu-154s **Leonid Faerberg** Transport-Photo Images

Belavia Tu-154M still active at Minsk National as recently as June 2014 **Simon De Rudder**

■ Czech Air Force 0601 awaits a visit to the paint shop **Tom Singfield**

■ Pakistan was a viable export market for the Tu-154 including flag carrier PIA **Colin Ballantine via Tom Singfield**

■ Syria was an export market for plenty of Soviet metal including this Tu-154M YI-AIA, Athens June 1985 **Richard Vandervord**

A pair of Tu-154Bs await their next missions on behalf of Balkan Bulgarian in the airline's modish final scheme Mark J Nutter

An evening departure aboard a Balkan Holidays Tu-154M Mark J Nutter

Cleared for takeoff Mark J Nutter

has a greater (by 15 percent) energy density, and creates very low toxic emissions (no sulphur or corrosive sulpher oxide) and can be used as fuel when supercooled as Liquid Natural Gas (LNG). Liquid hydrogen (LH2), while not a naturally occuring element on Earth, has three times the energy density, zero emissions, and theoretically at least, is totally renewable.

The Soviet Academy Of Sciences joined forces with other industrial research and development entities to work on creating hydrogen-fuelled transport, including in the aerospace sector, with a view to creating hypersonic aircraft and spacecraft. Research began under the name Kholod (Kh. for short, "Cold" in English) at the OKB-23 Myasishchev design bureau with an Il-76Kh. The programme and the fruits of the initial test flying was moved to the Tupolev bureau and much of CCCP-85035, a Tu-154 sans *suffixe*, was rebuilt including the installation of a heavily-insulated cryogenic fuel tank in the passenger cabin from the overwing exits all the way to the rear pressure dome in the tail. The tank could hold 20 square metres of LH2 at -253C or LNG at -162C feeding a specially installed Kuznetsov NK-88 turbofan engine in the centre number two position. The fuel was introduced by a cryogenic turbine pump on top of the engine into an annular heat exchanger downstream from the low pressure turbine which converted the fuel to a gaseous state (feeding a stable flow of liquid LH2 directly into the engine proved to be impossible). The NK-88 began static testing in February 1980, and a major cryogenic fuel facility was constructed at Zhukovskiy including cryogenic fuel trucks.

The first flight of the Tu-155 took place on April 15, 1988 under the command of Merited Test Pilot V. A. Sevan'kayev using LH2; in January 1989 the programme introduced LNG. The tank gave an endurance of two hours of flight and the performance of the engine was comparable to that of a conventional NK-8-2U running on oil-derived jet fuel. The Tu-155 made two trips abroad – one to Nice via Bratislava and one to the ILA 1990 air

Refuelling a Tu-154 in Novosibirsk

Gleb Osokin Transport-Photo Images

The Tu-155 cryogenic fuel testbed — Bernie Leighton

show at Hannover where the aircraft was the star of the show. Deutsch Airbus made a deal to share the fruits of the research to power a new version of the widebody Airbus A300. Limited funds as the Soviet Union was dismantled meant that Tu-155's last public performance was as part of the static display at the MosAeroShow 1992, after which the aircraft was placed in storage at Zhukovskiy where it remains to this day, having performed over 100 test flights and set fourteen world records, after contributing greatly to the understanding of the creation, storage and use of such unconventional fuels, and creating new test standards and safety and fire rules for cryogenic fuel aircraft.

The post-Soviet incarnation of Aeroflot inherited 44 Tu-154s. They were flown intensively throughout the nineties and into the twenty-first century, even as Airbus and Boeing narrowbodies joined the airline. The latest livery, heavy on silver paint, was developed in partnership with western branding agencies and Airbus Industrie but applied to the Tu-154 with great affect. A new two-class interior seating 24 passengers in business class and 102 in economy for a total of 126 was designed by Russian aerospace company AKKO to bring the comfort levels up to contemporary standards. The first airframe to be updated was unveiled at Aeroflot's Sheremeteyvo maintenance facility on October 31, 2000. Even as the Tu-154 was entering its twilight at Aeroflot, cheaply acquired, low time airframes were added to the fleet, and Tu-154 utilisation reached nearly ten hours a day per aircraft. A cheap purchase price and an abundance of spares from decommissioned aircraft could not mitigate the type's heavy fuel consumption and flagging public acceptance as time wore on, and the last scheduled Aeroflot flight operated by a Tu-154 took place as SU736 from Ekaterinburg to Moscow on December 31, 2009. Truly, this was the end of an era for Russian civil aviation.

For the rest of Russia's post-Soviet airlines, the Tu-154 was the backbone of the country through the 1990s, and even as late as 2007 made up a third of the airlines' fleets. Dozens of operators popped up in the first flush of economic freedom, some short-lived and obscure (Aerovolga, Kogalymavia, Perm Airlines, Yamal Airlines) and others reasonably well-known (KMV, Atlant-Soyuz, Bashkirian Airlines, Kras Air, Transaero, UTAir, Sibair which later rebranded as S7). Many were created from former Babyflots (eg. Baikal Airlines was previously the Siberian CAD; Donavia was previously the North Caucasian CAD based at Rostov-on-Don; and Omskavia was previously the West Siberian CAD, among others). Even the Uluyanovsk Higher Civil Aviation Flying School, whose fleet of 13 Tu-154Bs had seats in the back traditionally occupied by airsick cadet pilots waiting their turn while their classmates heaved the big beast around the circuit, got into the

A Tu-154 with one owner its whole life, Aeroflot; delivered January 1990 and retired December 2009   **Guy Viselé**

airline business, operating charter flights for local dignitaries, tour groups, sports teams and import businesses to destinations as far afield as Dubai.

As the years rolled on, the Russian airline business consolidated; airlines either went big time or went away. Alas, as their operations became more corporate, the last of the Soviet era hardware evaporated. Today only a handful of Tu-154s remain active – Alrosa Air Enterprise operate a pair of Tu-154Ms as the runways at their mining communities are too rugged for western hardware; Air Koryo keep a pair of antique Tu-154Bs (*nee* As) on flight status as a *de facto* strategic reserve air fleet and log occasional domestic passenger flights; and the Russian air force have a mixed fleet used to transport troops or perform other government duties.

The total number of Tu-154s built number 923, the biggest production run of any pure jet-powered airliner in the Soviet Union or Russia. To this day, half of all the passengers who have ever flown on Aeroflot (for decades the world's biggest airline) flew on the Tupolev Tu-154 – an incredible achievement that puts the type in the uppermost ranks of the most important transport aircraft ever built.

Slovakia's head of state Tu-154M shows off for the camera   **Dietmar Schreiber**

■ On September 7, 2010, Alrosa Tu-154M RA-85684 suffered a complete loss of electrical systems en route from Polyarny to Moscow, leaving only 3,300 kilos (7,300 lbs) of useable fuel. The disused airfield of Izhma was their only hope, and after two low passes to check the condition of the only 1,325 metre runway, made a miraculous landing, running off the end at low speed. All passengers were uninjured, and the aircraft returned to service. **Artyom Kuzhlev**

■ A hardworking Gazpromavia Tu-154M crew at sunrise **Artyom Kuzhlev**

B. Korzin Transport-Photos Images

Yakovlev Yak-40 & -42
The unsung heroes

The 1990s and 2000s saw a revolution in the airline world, especially in North America: the "regional jet", which evolved out of biz jets developed by Canadair in Quebec and Embraer in Brazil. This was the ultimate realisation of the airline network planners' dream of achieving two things that were difficult to do with a Boeing 737 or Airbus A320 – feed big hubs with traffic flows from the smallest outstations at jet speed, or in the case of medium-sized spokes, increase frequency from once or twice a day to half a dozen, outflying any competitor.

There had been a few attempts to do so earlier in the jet age, mostly by European airframers such as British Aerospace with the BAe 146 (which evolved into the Avro Regional Jet), the Fokker F-28 Fellowship (which evolved into the F-70 and F-100) and the unsuccessful VFW-614 (despite an innovative engine placement above the wing which reduced noise over the ground, only ten were sold). However, the birthplace of the regional jet was indisputably the Soviet Union, back in the 1960s.

I. Yak-40

The Yakovlev OKB had aspirations to build civil airliners as early as 1938 with the Yak-19 six-seater, followed by the Yak-8 and Yak-16, none of which went into production. It wasn't until the Tupolev Tu-104 and Tu-124 had proved the case for the jet engine that Yakovlev's chance came along. With major airports served by the Tu-104 and smaller provincial destinations by the Il-18 turboprop, there remained a galaxy of small and remote settlements across the eleven time zones of the Soviet Union that were candidates for fast and efficient air travel, instead of the reliable but slow and primitive Lisunov Li-2 (Douglas DC-3s built under licence), Ilyushin Il-12 and -14, and the Antonov An-2.

A joint directive was passed by the Communist Party Central Committee and the Council Of Ministers on April 30, 1965 to develop a small jetliner for operations into the smallest and most basic of airfields, including even grass

Kazakh Yak-40s gather at Osh Airport, October 1 1974
Lev Polikashin

CCCP-87351 was delivered to Aeroflot as CCCP-87351, seen at the ILA airshow, Hannover May 3, 1976   Guy Viselé

runways. Because the directive specified a takeoff distance as short as 700 metres (2,300 feet), various configurations were considered including a vertical takeoff and landing (VTOL) option. In the end, three Ivchenko AI-25s, each able to produce 1,500 kbp (3,310 lbst) of thrust, were arrayed around the tail, with one mounted on either side of the rear fuselage and the middle engine buried in the rear of the fuselage, fed by an S-duct directly under the vertical stabiliser, in the style of the day, as adopted by the Tu-154, the Hawker Siddeley Trident and the Boeing 727. This would provide an impressive thrust-to-weight ratio needed for short field performance, plus a useful amount of redundancy in the event of an engine failure. For operational autonomy at ill-equipped airfields, an Ivchenko AI-9 auxiliary power unit (APU) was added to provide electrical power and climate control on the ground, and compressed air for engine start.

The first prototype Yak-40, NATO reporting name Codling, was hand-built at MMZ no. 115 at Khodynka airfield in Moscow, and given the custom registration of CCCP-1966. It first flew on October 21, 1966 with test pilots A. L. Kolosov and Yu. B. Petrov at the controls. Four more prototypes joined the test programme, along with the first three preproduction machines off the line at Aviation Plant no. 292 at Saratov on the Volga River in southwest Russia. Improvements were made to each successive prototype, such as the addition of a service door on one, and a more pointed nosecone from the third aircraft onwards. The first three had a hatch behind the nose gear for pilots to bail out in midair in an emergency such as an unrecoverable spin. After an uneventful test programme, the type was certified in mid-1968 and operated its first flight for Aeroflot on September 30.

As production continued, various modifications to the design were made, such as removing the bullet fairing at the top of the tail, and adding or subtracting passenger windows depending on internal configurations. In 1969 a reverse thrust clamshell was added to the centre engine to shorten the ground run after landing. The mechanism was designed by the Yakovlev OKB, not Ivchenko, as it was considered part of the rear fuselage, rather than of the engine itself. Ivchenko themselves were not resting, as the AI-25 was soon uprated to deliver 1,750 kgp (3,860 lbst) of thrust. Incorporating these enhancements, CCCP-87791 was demonstrated at the 1971 Paris Air Show with a new 40-seat passenger interior.

Due to political hurdles and incompatible certification and operation documentation, Soviet airliners struggled to find export markets outside the immediate and obvious markets such as

UN-88271 served five different Kazah airlines, including Irtysh Avia out of the old capital of Almaty Richard Vandervord

Aerocaribbean's Yak-40 CU-T1220 previously served Cubana and went on to fly for East West in Chile and Oriental de Aviacion Venezuela at the end of the 1990s Tom Singfield

Yak-40EC registered I-JAKE flying for Air Settanta in June 1972 Tom Singfield

Yak-40FG D-BOBC (ex D-COBC) was one of six to serve domestic ports with General Air from a base at Hamburg, later became CCCP-87819, D2-EAG, I-JAKO and D2-EAG, seen in Brussels on April 9 1974 **Guy Viselé**

Warsaw Pact nations in eastern Europe, plus North Korea and Cuba. The Yak-40 was an exception to this, with impressively wide acceptance around the world. This is in part due to the innovative nature of the machine – the Yak-40 was decades ahead of its time by offering jet service to small communities.

A sole Yak-40E (for export) was delivered to Hungary as HA-YLR for use as a navaids calibrator, then in 1971 three Yak-40ECs (export, Collins) were delivered to Italian commuter airline Aertirrena with Collins avionics and radios. Five Yak-40FGs (Federal Germany) were sold to General Air of West Germany. Ultimately, export customers for 130 Yak-40s sold outside the Soviet Union were found in Afghanistan, Angola, Bulgaria, Cambodia, Cuba, Czechoslovakia, Equatorial Guinea, Ethiopia, both Germanys, Guatemala, Honduras, Hungary, Italy, Laos, Madagascar, the Philippines, Poland, Syria, Vietnam, Yugoslavia and Zambia.

Two main variations were worthy of a subtype designation. The Yak-40K was a cargo or combi variant that was produced from 1975 onwards, with a main deck side cargo door on the left side ahead of the wing. The first Yak-40K prototype, CCCP-87597, was converted from a regular passenger airframe and reregistered CCCP-87490.

The Yak-40D was an aftersales customisation available from the Smolensk Aircraft Plant which added two integral fuel tanks to the wings which added 1,600 kilograms (3,530 pounds) of fuel for a total fuel weight of six tons (13,230 pounds), increasing range from 1,200 kilometres (746 miles) to 2,500 km (1,554 miles).

As well as flying passengers on scheduled trips and government missions, the Yak-40 found

Two different versions of the CSA corporate brand resting between flights in Prague in March 1990 **Tom Singfield**

Jak-40LL Flight Research Institute in Prague **Jozef Tóth**

A rare air-to-air photo shoot with a Slovak Government Yak-40   Dietmar Schrieber

many specialised roles, such CCCP-87937, the sole Yak-40 Akva (Aqua) weather research aircraft, used for atmospheric studies and cloud-seeding (to provoke rainfall) out of its base in Ukraine (later converted to normal passenger operations). CCCP-87992 Yak-40 Schtorm (Sea Storm), CCCP-87536 Yak-40 Liros, and CCCP-87537 Yak-40 Meteo had similar weather research roles, whereas CCCP-87304 Fobos was used by the Lavochkin Science And Production Association for research in missile and space technology.

The Czechoslovakian aviation establishment had their own Yak-40 flying testbed, known locally as the Jak-40LL. It was most famously used for airborne trials of the Motorlet / Walter M-602 turboprop engine, installed in the

The interior of Vologda Air's RA-88231, a "Model T Ford" Yak-40 en route to Moscow VKO   Simon De Rudder

Yak-40K of Vologda Air delivered to Aeroflot in 1977, enjoying a low level acceleration after takeoff — **Artyom Kuzhlev**

AeroBratsk operate charter flights with a trio of Yak-40s out of their eponymous hometown; this one was delivered to Aeroflot in January 1976 amd also served Kolpashevo Air, Tomskavia and Ak Bars Aero — **Artyom Kuzhlev**

The cockpit of Vologda Air's Yak-40K RA-87905 — Robert Szymczak

An ex-CSA Yak-40 served the United Nations in 1991/92 before flying for Odessa Airlines in Ukraine, then in the Republic of Congo until retirement and storage at Point Noire — **Richard Vandervord**

LZ-DOF served four carriers, all on the Bulgarian register; flag carrier Balkan, regional Hemus Air, and two Albanian airlines — **Richard Vandervord**

nose of OK-EEA in development for use on the Let L-610 commuter airliner project. The Polish air force used four of their 18 Yak-40s for target towing from a 3,000 metre (9,840 feet) cable that could be extended from a drum in the rear fuselage.

But it was flying passengers that the Yak-40 did best. By 1980 the Yak-40 was serving a head-spinning 276 destinations with Aeroflot alone; by the time production ended at Saratov in November 1981, 1,013 airframes had been built, making it the Soviet Union's biggest-selling jetliner.

The Yak-40 remained in frontline passenger service for years after the end of production – there simply wasn't other type that could fill the role. By the time Aeroflot began retiring the type in 1993, the airline's fleet of baby Yakovlevs had carried 354 million passengers. As late as 2016, Yak-40s can be found in the backwaters of Russia and Ukraine, still flying on bookable scheduled services, and with VIP interiors in private hands flying as executive jets.

The first revenue Yak-42 arrives at Krasnodar B. Korzin Transport-Photo Images

Yak-42 RA-42427 in Krasnodar Valentin Grebnev Transport-Photo Images

II. YAK-42

Two upgrades of the Yak-40 were considered. The Yak-40P was a long haul version, with a 1,000 litre (220 imperial gallon) fuel tank in a fairing extending forward of each wing. The other was the Yak-40M; a scale model was produced which included a fuselage stretch to accommodate up to 44 passengers, slats on the leading edge of the wing, and main landing gear with two wheels on each strut instead of one.

Although these did not reach prototype stage, there was room for a bigger, faster machine which came to be branded the Yak-42, NATO reporting name Clobber, in a niche identified by Aeroflot as early as 1972, to replace the Ilyushin Il-18, Antonov An-24 and early-build Tupolev Tu-134s. Yakovlev's initial proposal was a 114-seater with a straight wing, powered by two Solviev D-30s. However, the need to improve fuel burn pushed Yakovlev towards the utilisation of three high-bypass Lotarev D-36s, rated at 6,500 kgp (14,330 lbst). The wing sweep started at almost zero on the drawing board, before reaching 11 degrees by the time the first prototype, CCCP-1974, was built at Khodyna and test flown for the first time on March 7, 1975.

The wing shape was still found to be less than optimal and a whole new wing design was created for the second prototype, CCCP-1975, with a sweepback of 23 degrees, as well as a longer passenger cabin. CCCP-1976 had beefed-up deicing and other minor additions. CCCP-1977 was used for testing unusual attitude recovery and to explore incipient spin characteristics. During the test programme it sported a spin-recovery parachute in a fairing above the centre engine.

Production began at Saratov alongside Yak-40s in April 1978 starting with CCCP-42300. The certification process was completed at the end of November 1980 and the Yak-42 entered airline service with Aeroflot from Moscow to Krasnodar on December 22, 1980.

Yak-42s rolled off the line much slower than planned, with only ten machines produced up to mid-1981. A second production line was opened up at the Smolensk Aircraft Plant, although a total of

The interior of a Yak-42 as it hums along on another scheduled flight — **B. Korzin** Transport-Photo Images

Cockpit of Yak-42D RA-42427 — **Anton Bannikov**

Yak-42 cabin at the time the type was introduced to service in 1980 — **B. Korzin** Transport-Photo Images

After a career in the 1980s with Aeroflot, LY-AAU went to Lithuanian Airlines aka flyLAL, and ended her days with Cubana as CU-T1246, seen at London Heathrow in March 1994 **Richard Vandervord**

Donbassaero's UR-42308, one of 14 Yak-42s operated out of its base at Donetsk, seen at Moscow Domodedovo **Richard Vandervord**

This Ukrainian Yak-42 UR-42376 was leased to Macedonian Airlines December 1993, between flights in Zurich **Charles Bargibant**

A 1990-build Yak-42D of Volga Air Express blasts out of Sochi **Fyodor Borisov** Transport-Photo Images

This Yak-42 enjoys a refreshing mid-winter nightstop at Moscow DME. It was delivered to Aeroflot in 1984 and retired by Saratov Airlines at the end of 2016; who still fly seven others **Artyom Kuzhlev**

Izhavia retain a fleet of nine active Yak-42Ds operating out of their base at Izhevsk **Simon De Rudder**

only eight airframes were built there. Small changes continued to be made, such as deleting the bullet fairing at the leading edge of the top of the tail in an echo of the development of its smaller sibling; on the Yak-42 this was later substituted with a kink to help reduce airflow separation. In the course of 1981, Aeroflot's very small fleet of Yak-42s carried 200,000 passengers on domestic services out of Moscow, plus some second-tier international flying such as Leningrad to Helsinki and Donetsk to Prague.

Despite a slow start, the future for the Soviet Union's new trijet were bright, with excellent passenger acceptance and very favourable operating economics thanks to the high-bypass turbofan engines.

Alas, disaster struck on June 28, 1982. Aeroflot 8641 was a scheduled flight from Leningrad to Kiev, operated by CCCP-42529. Midway to its destination, as it passed high over the city of Mayr in southeast Belarus, the aircraft violently pitched into an unrecoverable dive beyond vertical, leading to an inflight breakup; wreckage was strewn across the Belorussian countryside. There were no survivors among the 124 passengers and eight crew.

The fleet was immediately grounded and a painstaking investigation found the problem – metal fatigue in the jackscrew that controlled the angle of attack of the horizontal stabiliser. When the jackscrew failed, the entire horizontal tail separated from the aircraft, rendering it completely unflyable (the same scenario brought down Alaska 261 in 2000, a McDonnell Douglas MD-80, not to mention fictitious "Southjet 227" in the 2012 movie *Flight* starring Denzel Washington).

The investigation and replacement of jackscrews in all Yak-42s was time-consuming, and the type did not return to the skies for two years, getting back into passenger service in October 1984. The type's reputation and sales prospects were damaged, although the type demonstrated excellent reliability and efficiency for the rest of the decade. The production target of 2,000 airframes fell out of reach, never to return.

In 1991 the definitive variant emerged, the Yak-42D. The main difference with the Yak-42 *sans suffixe* was an extra 3,100 litres (682 imperial gallons) of fuel tank capacity which extended the aircraft's range. By the time production ended,

KrasAvia's Yak-42D back in Russia after six years in Iran with Fars Air Qeshm — Artyom Anikeev

Iran was a major operator of Russian hardware, and Fars Air Qeshm was a longtime Yak-42 operator; EP-QFB (ex ER-YCF) served for seven years and seen just after touchdown at Tehran Mehrabad on November 15 2009 **Guy Viselé**

125 Yak-42Ds had been produced out of a total production run of 180 aircraft.

Despite the rocky start and consequent lack of mainstream success, the Yak-42 proved itself in service. Export sales were achieved with the sale of four to Cubana and eight to China General Aviation. In the aftermath of the breakup of the Soviet Union, several republics inherited Yak-42s, adding Lithuania (Lithuanian Airlines), Ukraine (Donbassaero and Aerosvit), Kazakhstan (SCAT) and Armenia (Armavia) to the list of countries that operated the type. Pakistan's Aero Asia operated a total of nine at different times, all on lease from Tulpar Air over a period of around five years beginning at the turn of the century.

Iran's Fars Air Qeshm namechecked an island in the Straits Of Hormuz but in reality was based at the Tehran's downtown Mehrabad airport and used a selection of Ukrainian-flagged Yak-42Ds to maintain service to Kermanshah, Ahvaz, Mashhad and Khorramabad between 2003 and 2013. Iran was famous for leasing a large number of Russian planes to fill the capacity gap left by sanctions that inhibited its ability to buy new western jets, although the experience was not incredibly positive, with a dismal series of fatal accidents involving Tu-154s and an Il-62. The loss of Caspian 7908 in July 2009 was the final straw, and the Tu-154 was banned from Persian skies, leaving the Yak-42 as the last Russian-built jet to fly in Iran.

In Russia, major operators of the Yak-42 included Kuban Airlines, Izhavia, UTAir, KrasAvia, Grozny-Avia, Polet Airlines, Centre-Avia, and Saratov Airlines. A low profile bird even in its heyday, dozens remain in service at the time of writing.

III. Yak-242 & the MC-21

In 1989, a major update of the Yak-42, to be dubbed the Yak-42M, went through the planning stages. It was to feature a fuselage stretch of 4.62 metres (15 feet 2 inches) accommodating 156 passengers, plus new wings with winglets and a supercritical profile. The powerplant was to be the Muravchenko D-436M, based on the Lotarev D-36 but uprated to provide 7,500 kgp (16,540 lbst) at maximum power. In the cockpit would be the same advanced suite of digital avionics as on the Tupolev Tu-204, and fly-by-wire control surfaces.

This incarnation of the Yak-42M did not reach prototype stage, and nor did the next version, which moved engines one and three out from the side of the fuselage to pylons under the wings – a Lockheed L-1011 lookalike, like early Tu-204 design studies. The centre engine in the tail was then deleted and what remained was a twin-engined narrowbody with a resemblance to the Airbus A320 and Boeing 737. This design was mated to the latest wing technology emerging in the 1990s from

TsAGI, and the Lotarev D-36 engines were swapped out in favour of Aviadvigatel PS90As.

The updated design was named the Yak-242 and construction of prototypes was envisioned for 1995 and entry into service for 1997. In fact financial difficulties and other hardships in the early years of post-Soviet industry in Russia rendered those dates wishful thinking and the project was shelved.

As the instability of the decade that began with the end of the Soviet Union receded, the remaining assets of a once-great aircraft-building nation, both human, technical and financial, began to reform and renew; on February 20, 2006, President Vladimir Putin issued Presidential Decree No. 140 which merged shares in the old OKBs - Tupolev, Ilyushin, Irkut, Mikoyan, Sukhoi, Ilyushin and Yakovlev - to create a new joint-stock company: United Aircraft Corporation. Initially the civilian product line was all inherited: Tupolev Tu-204, Ilyushin Il-96.

And the work to create the stillborn Yak-242 was not in vain. As Russia's economic situation stabilised then began to improve at the start of the new century, the aerospace industry consolidated and rationalised. The Russian Aerospace Agency Rosaviakosmos announced the need for a new short and medium haul mainliner in 2002; in mid-2003 the union of Yakovlev and Ilyushin resurrected the Yak-242 and this design was declared the winner of the tender. The new machine was renamed the Irkut MC-21 (which refers to "Magistralny Samolyot 21 veka" – airliner of the twenty-first century). On May 28, 2017, the first MC-21, registration 73051, lauched on its first flight, and is now test flying along with a second prototype; entry into service (EIS) is planned for early 2020 with launch customer Iraero, and demand over ten years to number 1,000 aircraft. The order book presently stands at 205, all Russian carriers save Cairo Aviation, a loyal Tu-204 operator.

With the full backing of the state and the rest of the aviation hierarchy in Russia, the MC-21 is a product line of three different models with three different fuselage sizes: the MC-21-200 is the equivalent of the Airbus A319 or Boeing 737-700, the MC-21-300 is the equivalent of the A320 or 737-800, and the MC-21-400 is the equivalent of the A321 or 737-900. The MC-21-300 is the most popular variant, representing the majority of orders from Aeroflot, UTAir, Red Wings and Cairo Aviation.

The Irkut MC-21 and the Sukhoi Superjet 100 represent the new Russian civil aviation industry and have in their DNA one hundred years of cutting edge aerospace development, some of which is told in these pages. What will the next chapter bring?

Irkut MC-21-300 landing at Zhukovsky — Artyom Anikeev

Artyom Anikeev

Ilyushin Il-86 & -96
The peoplemovers

The jet age boom in Soviet skies meant that by the end of the 1960s, the airways were congested. Aeroplanes had to queue to takeoff and circle in holding patterns waiting to land. Similar problems in the West led to the early 1970s march of jumbo jets, beginning with the Boeing 747 entering service in January 1970 with Pan Am, soon followed by the McDonnell Douglas DC-10 in August 1971 with American Airlines and United Airlines, the Lockheed L-1011 Tristar in April 1972 with Eastern Airlines, and the Airbus A300 in May 1974 with Air France.

The design bureaux of the Soviet Union set out to create a people mover that would not only reduce the number of aircraft movements needed to serve a busy route, but also reduce cost per seat with improved fuel efficiency and lower operating costs, which would enable more people to fly for an affordable price.

I. Il-86

A specific design brief was issued by the authorities at the end of the 1960s: the new so-called *aerobus* should be able to lift 40 tons (80,000 pounds) of payload including 350 passengers off a 2,600 metre (8,530 feet) runway and fly for 3,600 kilometres (2,237 miles).

The Ilyushin OKB offered a stretched Il-62M-250 but the design bureau with an early lead was Antonov, with a double-decker passenger version of their massive turboprop-powered An-22 military transport. Going forward, however, Antonov fell out of political favour in the post-Khrushchev era whereas Ilyushin's standing improved.

On September 8, 1969, the Council of Ministers' Presidium Commission on Defence Industry Matters chose the Ilyushin OKB to develop the *aerobus*. Double-decker configurations were discarded due to their heavy structural weight; a single deck also made regular passenger loading as well as emergency evacuation much more straightforward. The final, circular-cross section widebody fuselage was 6.08 metres (11 feet 11 inches) in diameter which would allow comfortable nine abreast seating and the carriage of two side-by-side LD3 containers in the cargo bays beneath.

On March 9, 1972, the Council of Ministers issued a directive ordering the commencement of work on the Il-86, with flight testing to begin in 1976 and entry into service to follow before the 1980 Olympic Games in Moscow. The next three years were spent breathing life into a configuration closely resembling the Il-62, with four Soloviev D-30KU low-bypass turbofans affixed in pairs to the rear fuselage beneath a high T-tail. By 1975 however, no amount of massaging the weight of the proposed *aerobus* or the efficiency of its wing could hide the fact that four D-30s simply couldn't

Il-86 and its crew **Valentin Grebnev** Transport-Photo Images

The first revenue flight of the Il-86 arrives at Tashkent, December 26 1980 **B. Korzin** Transport-Photo Images

provide enough thrust to guarantee sustained flight with an engine failure during a maximum weight takeoff.

The only engine suitable for a civilian application that could do the job was the Kuznetsov NK-8, which was customised for the *aerobus* to create the NK-86, capable of pushing out 13,000 kgp (28,665 pounds) of thrust, albeit with the very high fuel consumption of three tons (6,610 pounds) of fuel per engine per hour. With jet fuel at the time going cheap, and the aircraft intended only for short and medium haul trips, this was acceptable and the Council of Ministers amended their directive on March 26, 1975 to kick off development of an NK-86 powered machine.

Another competing solution to the Soviet airline capacity shortfall was to look abroad. In fact one reason the Il-86 had a long ten year gestation was partly due to some long pauses in development as foreign aircraft types came into fashion with industry elites in the Soviet Union, then slipped out of reach due to political obstacles; only then would work on the Il-86 programme restart. An early favourite was the Boeing 747, for which Aeroflot made repeated acquisition attempts over the next two or three decades, but the climate was never right – in the 1970s there were too many trade barriers between the Soviet Union and the USA, and in the 1980s and especially the 1990s the Soviet Union was suffering economically, so by the time the political obstacles had melted away, the 747 was too much aeroplane for Aeroflot's commercial requirements.

What made it easier for Boeing to back out of a sale to a controversial country was that the order book for their jumbo was pretty healthy, whereas Lockheed, late to the party with the L-1011, needed to sell some aeroplanes (in the end, Lockheed only produced 250 L-1011s versus 446 DC-10s, and over 1,500 747s).

On March 11, 1974, an L-1011 touched down in Moscow for three days of demonstration flights and sales presentations. The Soviets were impressed and wanted to buy 30 L-1011-250s and build another 100 under licence in Russia. This was pursued by both sides but by 1978 US president Jimmy Carter's administration began counting human rights as a factor in foreign policy and trade decisions. Technology export requests were denied, and this also scotched hopes of a long-

■ Promotional photos from 1980   **Aeroflot**

View from the flight deck aboard RA-86125 as it maneouvres to land at Antalya **Fyodor Borisov** Transport-Photo Images

Flight engineer's station
Fyodor Borisov Transport-Photo Images

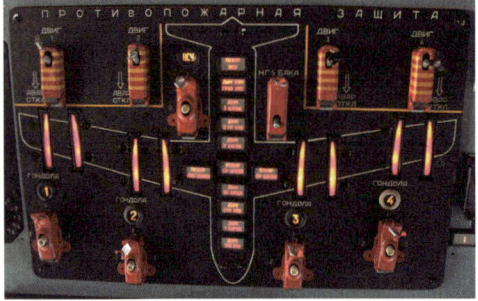

Fire detection system in the flight deck of RA-86125
Fyodor Borisov Transport-Photo Images

range Il-86 powered by General Electric CF6-50s.

Still, attempts were made to utilise a foreign powerplant – or elements thereof. A 1976 trade mission visited Rolls-Royce in Derby, England, with the intention of buying eight engines to reverse-engineer. Rolls, however, had learned from their experience of sharing their Nene engine technology with the Kirill Klimov OKB in the late 1940s that had resulted in the Klimov VK-1 which powered the MiG-15; this time, Rolls insisted the sale had to be for more than 100 engines.

From the very beginning, the Il-86 was designed to work with the existing infrastructure of Soviet airports, some of which were small and basic. 300 passengers turning up at once would, in some provincial locales, overwhelm airport facilities, especially with baggage handling. Various innovations were considered, including the possibility of all baggage travelling with its owner right next to the passenger seat or in unusually spacious overhead lockers. However all variations on this theme meant a longer passenger cabin

Aeroflot's CCCP-86008 demonstrates its built-in air stairs B. Korzin Transport-Photo Images

due to space taken up by baggage, as well as safety concerns in a high-G event.

The baggage solution that was chosen ended up becoming one of the Il-86's signature characteristics. Passengers would board from the tarmac via three sets of integral metal airstairs to enter the aircraft on the lower deck, finding themselves in a spacious lobby lined with shelves for their bags. Having dropped off what wasn't needed on the voyage, passengers would then climb internal stairs into the main deck passenger cabin with their hand luggage. This not only reduced the need for sophisticated ground handling equipment but also sped up turnaround times and had a direct impact on the Il-86's economic efficiency. It was dubbed the 'luggage at hand' system.

The main deck was wide enough for a typical passenger configuration of nine abreast in three blocks of three seats. (Incidentally this was a cabin layout almost never used aboard contemporary nine-abreast widebodies of the West, where a 2-5-2 layout was the norm in a nine-abreast configuration; alas widebodies of today have followed their Soviet predecessor and are almost all 3-3-3; the days of cosy seat pairs for couples seem to have ended.)

The main deck had four ICAO type I exits on each side, with an inflatable two-abreast emergency evacuation chute fixed to each. Seats were of a new design – gone were the thin Soviet-style seats found in most Tupolevs; these were plusher, wider, and had a number of innovations in the seatback, such as a discrete map light to cast a small pool of light downwards, a switchable ducted fan to cool off, and an integral oxygen mask, all of which did away with the need for overhead Passenger Service Units (PSUs).

TsAGI performed a heroic amount of research to help create a wing that was not only highly efficient in cruise but also would enable safe low-speed flight to enable the best possible short-field performance. The sophisticated leading edge slats and triple-slotted trailing edge

■ The stairs leading to the lower deck entrance aboard an Atlant-Soyuz Il-86   **Fyodor Borisov** Transport-Photo Images

■ Lower deck   **Fyodor Borisov** Transport-Photo Images

Il-86 of Pulkovo Airlines arriving at Petropavlovsk — Sam Chui

flaps represented the cutting edge of aeronautical engineering of the era, but the biggest departure from the past was the placement of engines.

The story goes that Boeing's chief engineer Joe Sutter and the head of the Ilyushin OKB, Genrikh Novozhilov, met in Paris in 1971 during the Air Salon and in an unofficial exchange of technology, Novozhilov revealed valuable information about the use of titanium in airframes and components, and Sutter sketched on the tablecloth the basics of pylon-mounted engines and aeroelastic wings. The tablecloth went back to Russia with Novozhilov and bore fruit when the Il-86 became the first Soviet-produced airliner to have engines mounted on underwing pylons, a configuration that had long been dismissed by prevailing wisdom in the Soviet Union; the wing-pylon engine placement on the B-47, B-52, 707 and 747 was looked down upon as inferior. Soviet dogmatism held that problems had immutable, "scientifically-correct" solutions, so breaking away to find new ways of doing things took courage.

The first Il-86 prototype, CCCP-86000, was built at Ilyushin's research facility at Khodynka airfield in Moscow, along with a second airframe for static testing. On December 22, 1976, 86000 took to the air for the first time, under the command of a Hero Of The Soviet Union, Merited Test Pilot Edward I. Kuznetsov. He was joined by first officer G. N. Volokhov, flight engineer I. N. Yakimets, and navigator V. A. Shchotkin. The landing took place at nearby Zhukovsky airfield, the home of Soviet aviation test flying.

The Il-86 made its international debut in June 1977 at the Paris Air Show where it was given a positive reception by the world's aviation community, and a NATO reporting name, Camber. Production was assigned to the Ministry of Aircraft Manufacture plant no. 64 at Voronezh (later known as VASO). The plant lacked capacity, as did much of the civil sector of the Soviet aerospace industry at that time, as a large-scale military aircraft boom was in full swing and at the same time the economy was stagnating. The Polish State Aviation Works (PZL for short) was brought in to participate in a technology transfer which led to PZL producing the entire tail assembly (horizontal and vertical stabilisers, rear fuselage and tailcone), all control surfaces, and the engine pylons, and possibly the wing too. (The outsourcing of the wing never happened, as

Ramp check for Ural Airlines' 1990-build Il-86 at Yekaterinburg   **Sam Chui**

The Il-86 was not a huge export success but five machines served China Xinjiang Airlines including B-2016, seen resting between flights at its home base of Urumqi   **Richard Vandervord**

This 1993 Il-86 of Atlant Soyuz previously served Transaero, Krasair and VASO, scrapped at Moscow Vnukovo in 2011 **Guy Viselé**

UN-86068, originally delivered to Aeroflot in January 1985, resting at its home base of Almaty **Richard Vandervord**

Ural Airlines Il-86 interior; note the sense of space created by the absence of overhead bins above the centre seats **Sam Chui**

the visible elements of the political upheaval that would lead to the end of the communism in Europe had already begun in Poland, so Voronezh was instructed to keep control of the wing manufacture by the higher-ups, as it is the most technologically-sensitive element of any aeroplane design.)

The second prototype, CCCP-86001, was produced at Voronezh and first flew on October 24, 1977. Test flying was thorough, and even included incipient spinning, hence the installation of a spin recovery parachute in the tailcone in place of an APU. A route-proving trip to the Black Sea resort of Sochi took place on April 23, 1978, followed by sorties in September to Simferopol, Mineral'nyye-Vody, and back to Sochi. Manufacturer's trials were completed on October 20, 1978, and state certification began.

A third Il-86, the first true production machine, was registered CCCP-86002 and first flown on March 2, 1979. Minister for Civil Aviation Boris P. Bugayev signed to authorise the commencement of the state acceptance trials on April 24, 1979, briefly interrupted in June when CCCP-86000 went to the Paris Air Show. On September 23, the third production airframe (and hence fifth overall) registered CCCP-86004 was ferried to Moscow Vnukovo in preparation for further route-proving outings, flying to Leningrad, Rostov-on-Don, and Tashkent.

Operational trials were completed on December 18, 1980, by which time 490 flights had been performed logging 1,221 hours and 49 minutes in the air. The next day prototype CCCP-86000 was flown to Kiev for use as an instructional airframe at the Kiev Institute of Civil Aviation Engineers (and resides today in the museum collection at Kiev Zhuliany airport).

The only incident of note in the development of the Il-86 was when the second production airframe suffered a serious engine fire in number four engine (right, outboard) after takeoff leaving Moscow Vnukovo on an Aeroflot acceptance shakedown flight. The danger was compounded when the flight engineer inadvertently shut down engine number one (left, outboard), then number four, leaving the heavy jet

Il-86s gather on the ramp at St Petersburg Pavel Novikov Transport-Photo Images

with only two functioning engines (two and three). With no time to spare, the captain rolled CCCP-86004 around a steep 180 degree turn and landed on the reciprocal runway. Some modifications were made to the NK-86 engine as a result of the fire - and no doubt to cockpit procedures too.

The type certificate was issued on December 24, 1980 in accordance with NLGS-2 regulations and the inaugural revenue flight followed on December 26 on the busy route from Moscow to Tashkent, exactly the kind of trip the Il-86 was intended for. The target of being in service for the 1980 Olympics had been missed, but better late than never, Soviet Union's first widebody was in passenger service. And it had been a mammoth undertaking from the start; for one thing, it was only the world's second widebody with four engines, following the Boeing 747. To express official approval, on April 22, 1981, a group of Ilyushin engineers were awarded the Lenin Prize for their work on the Il-86.

Domestic service within the Soviet Union gradually built up in the early part of 1981, with Novosibirsk, Alama-Ata and Mineral'nyye Vody seeing early scheduled service. On July 3, 1981, the Il-86 operated its first scheduled international flight along the axis of twentieth-century European socialism from Moscow to East Berlin, with service to Prague following on October 12 and Vienna on October 25.

To increase efficiency, a new 450-seat configuration was designated the Il-86V; the first of its kind was registered CCCP-86015 and entered service on proving flights from Moscow to Tashkent in April 1985.

Five militarised Il-86s were manufactured, redesigned as the Il-80 with the NATO reporting name of Maxdome, sometimes known as the Il-86VPU. These machines are used for national emergency airborne command post (NEACP) coordination, and have a large humped radome on the forward fuselage plus pods under the wing roots containing gas turbine-driven generators to run the extra hardware on board, which is also evident from airborne refuelling port on the left side of the nose, and the number of aerials and antennae that are

The Il-86VKP, also known as the Il-80, is an airborne command post; four were built and three remain in service out of Chkalovsky Air Base near Moscow
Sergey Lebedev

visible. The Il-80 prototype made its first flight on May 29, 1985 and four production machines, CCCP-86146, 47, 48 and 49 were all handed over after a short test programme.

The Il-86 was not an export sales success, mostly due to the inefficiency of the 1960s-era NK-86 engines. Also, airliner manufacturers of the West had learned to harness the clout of their banking system to provide credit to airlines, or for the banks to just own the jets outright and lease them to airlines, enabling even the most cash-strapped operator to afford state-of-the-art Western jets. The Soviet Union's economy by then was mired in the doldrums of late-empire sclerosis and couldn't begin to arrange similar terms.

Ultimately the only foreign customer for new-build Il-86s was China Xinjiang Airlines who took three machines to operate on domestic routes across the Middle Kingdom from their base at Urumqi in Xinjiang province. East Germany's Interflug was poised to add a pair of Il-86s and even went as far as allocating registrations DDR-AAA and -AAB; to this day the occasional framed poster or other promotional item can be found in junk shops on the east side of Berlin showing an Il-86 in Interflug's distinctive red livery. But by the mid 1980s, thawing of relations in a soon-to-be reunited Europe meant Interflug were able to acquire three Airbus A310s instead (DDR-ABA, -ABB and -ABC).

With the breakup of the Soviet Union in 1991, Il-86s wound up at some of the new airlines in newly-formed independent republics. Aeroflot's Kazakh CAD became Kazakhstan Airlines and with it came seven Il-86s; Armenian Airlines inherited two that had previously been part of Aeroflot's Yerevan operations; and Uzbekistan Airways began life with ten left behind by the retreat of the Soviet empire at their Tashkent hub. In addition, elements of Aeroflot's Russian operations split into Babyflots such as East Line, Orient Avia, AJT Air International, Atlant-Soyuz, Sibir (today S7), Pulkovo Airlines, Kras Air, Ural Airlines, Donavia, Russian Sky and others, all of whom operated secondhand Il-86s.

II. Il-96

With the Cold War at an end, and access to foreign technology no longer held hostage by politics, the Achilles Heel of the Il-86 could be addressed once again – its low tech engines and high fuel burn. The Ilyushin OKB and the Voronezh facility worked out how to incorporate the CFM International CFM56 engine, a wildly successful turbofan engine produced by a joint venture between General Electric of the USA and SNECMA of France. The engine is found on all Boeing 737s from the -300 series on, reengined KC-135s, all Airbus A340-200s and -300s, and some A320 aircraft. The CFM56-powered Ilyushin was designated the Il-86M and tooling was produced at Voronezh for the production of twenty aircraft.

However, there was already a new local aero engine on the drawing board at the Soloviev OKB, a true high-bypass powerplant intended to drive the next generation of Soviet jetliners, the D-90, initially conceived to power the Tupolev Tu-204 project. It was soon realised that using a common engine for an updated Il-86 would reduce costs. The Tu-204 was originally going to have a third engine buried in the tail, and a D-90 that would have powered the trijet would not be powerful enough for the new Il-86, but the request to update the thrust output of the D-90 was met with acclaim all round – not only would an uprated engine be able to power a new Il-86 but would also enable the Tu-204 to become a twin.

However, it soon appeared that even this would not be enough power, and with no further thrust to be had from the engine, the new bird had to be shrunk, with a new fuselage length that was five metres (16 feet 5 inches) shorter than the Il-86, allowing passenger accommodation for 300. The 'luggage at hand' system and lower deck airstairs were done away with, and the main deck had only three doors on each side, instead of four.

The new incarnation of the *aerobus* was considered sufficiently evolved to get a new branding, and was christened the Il-96, and the new engine was renamed the PS-90 (with the PS taken from the initials of the founder of the OKB, Pavel Aleksandrovich Solviev). Advanced design

■ RA-96011 comes in to land at Voronezh for a heavy check at VASO　　**Alexander Mishin** Transport-Photo Images

techniques gave Ilyushin a much greater degree of control on important issues such as structural weight and performance. TsAGI and Ilyushin worked together to create a new super-critical wing design, with the addition of inboard high speed ailerons and spoilers for improved roll control and, using new computer modelling, improvements to 'local' aerodynamics across the entire aerofoil. Most visibly, the Il-96 was fitted with winglets.

The cockpit incorporated major upgrades, including the introduction of a glass cockpit featuring CRT screens instead of gauges and fly-by-wire controls. A three-person flight crew was envisioned, although the engineer had no panel, creating a totally forward-facing cockpit.

The Il-96 was enjoying the same exact process that turned the DC-10 into the MD-11 or the 747 Classic into the 747-400: reduced flight crew, glass cockpit, fly-by-wire, big fan high-bypass powerplants, winglets. Sales for the Il-96 would prove hard to come by, but in technological terms the hard product was still very much in the game.

On December 1, 1986, the Ilyushin OKB submitted performance specifications in their presentation to the Ministry of Civil Aviation: maximum payload 40 tons (88,200 pounds) as part of an all-up weight of 216 tons (476,280 pounds), a range of 11,000 kilometres (6,837 miles), a cruise ceiling of 12,100 metres (39,700 feet) at a speed of 900 km/h (560 mph). This was met with approval and construction of the first prototype began at the Ilyushin research centre at Khodynka.

On September 28, 1988 CCCP-96000 flew for the first time, under the command of Ilyushin OKB's chief test pilot Stanislaw G. Briznyuk, a Hero Of The Soviet Union and Merited Test Pilot. Flight tests followed; the new machine was in some ways only an evolution of an existing design but incorporated many revolutionary elements and the test programme was demanding for all concerned, made much more complicated by the political certainties of the last 40 years coming to an end.

CCCP-96000 was publicly unveiled at the Aviation Day fly-past at Moscow Tushino on

Flight deck of Aeroflot Il-96 RA-96008 after a flight from Moscow to Istanbul   Marius Höpner

August 20, 1989. On November 11, second prototype CCCP-96001 rolled out of the factory and took to the air at Voronezh, joining the intensive test flying programme. Valentines Day 1990 saw the international debut of the Il-96 when CCCP-96001 performed an aerobatic display at the Asian Aerospace airshow in Singapore.

The first production Il-96, CCCP-96002, flew for the first time on July 9, 1990. This demonstrated that the Voronezh facility had mastered series production of the new type in a tight timeframe and was now able to commence deliveries to airline customers.

1991 saw further steps to certification including a two week stint in February in Yakutsk for cold weather trials (the elements cooperated, giving a cold soak down to -53C). November 21 and 22 saw second production airframe CCCP-96005 perform an 18 hour trip around Russia routing Moscow - Petropavlovsk - Kamchatsky - Moscow to check range and endurance. In 1992 the third production airframe, CCCP-96006, set off from Moscow and flew to Portland Oregon via the North Pole and Anchorage to mark the fifty-fifth anniversary of Valeriy P. Chkalov's record-breaking flight over the North Pole to the USA in a Tupolev ANT-25. From October 21 to 25, CCCP-96005 flew down to Melbourne in Australia to take part in Airshow Down Under.

Flight tests revealed that the Il-96 possessed excellent handling, stability and controllability characteristics, which made it an ideal candidate to form the baseline of a series of variations on the payload, range, and even the number of engines. The initial production version, therefore, was branded the Il-96-300.

The type certificate, in accord with the latest NLGS-3 standards, was granted on December 29, 1992, after 1,769 flights spanning 3,100 hours in the air. A series of further bureaucratic hurdles remained, however, and the Il-96-300 wasn't able to commence passenger flights until July 14, 1993, when the first passenger flight was operated from Moscow to New York JFK. Service to Barcelona and Madrid followed on July 31, Las Palmas on November 13, and London Heathrow on November

Pushback of Aeroflot Il-96 RA-96008 'Moiseyev' before another red-eye service to Yerevan　　　Robert Szymczak

Aeroflot's RA-96008 had a three year reprieve when it was acquired by Cubana in August 2014 and flew until September 2017 on tropical routes as CU-T1717 **Tim Bowrey**

Il-96PU Command Post in the livery of Rossiya **Artyom Kuzhlev**

A pair of Il-96s in the Sheremetyevo snow **Artyom Anikeev** Transport-Photo Images

Inflight on Aeroflot Il-96 RA-96010 from Moscow to Antalya — Simon De Rudder

14. Seoul, San Francisco, Seattle and Los Angeles came online in early 1994.

Later the same year, a new subsidiary of Aeroflot called ARIA (Aeroflot Russian International Airlines) was formed to provide Il-96-300 service, and this business unit went into action by launching service from Moscow to Buenos Aires via Sal (Cape Verde) on October 31, 1994, followed by Moscow to Sao Paolo via Larnaca, Sal and Rio on November 4. Moscow to Paris was taken over by the new flagship on May 25, 1995.

III. Il-96M & Il-96-400T

As early as November 1989, negotiations began for the development of Il-96s and Tu-204s to be fitted with Western engines and avionics. On December 7, 1990, a framework agreement was signed to lay the ground for a feasibility study to equip a stretched Il-96M with Pratt & Whitney PW2037 turbofans.

For a traditional organisation like the Ilyushin OKB to integrate design, workflow, and certification procedures with specialists from different countries, languages, alphabets and cultures represented a huge leap, but by no means an unbridgable one. Specialists from Russia and the USA were mutually acquainted with the special design features of the aeroplane, the engines and the avionics. Bilingual lists were drawn up of equipment delivery and installation dates, and technical hurdles gradually solved.

Russia's State Air Register and the US Federal Aviation Administration (FAA) jointly conceived a basis to certify the Il-96M, and on November 30, 1991, the first Il-96-300 prototype was flown into Khodynka to be converted to the first Il-96M. The fuselage was stretched by inserting two barrels, one ahead of the wing measuring 6.05 metres (19 feet 10 inches) and one behind the wing measuring 3.3 metres (10 feet 10 inches). Rockwell Collins avionics were fitted in the cockpit and PW2037 engines under the wings. Reregistered RA-96000, the converted aircraft was rolled out on March 29, 1993 and first flew on April 4.

The Il-96M was unveiled at the 1993 Paris Airshow, where Rockwell Collins test pilot Ross Wains flew it in aerobatic displays. It was also demonstrated at the MAKS-93 airshow between August 31 and September 5, and at Andrews AFB near Washington DC between November 6 and 17 1994. Another trip to Australia, this time to demonstrate the new Il-96M, came around in March 1995 for a return visit to Airshow Down Under. An export sales visit was paid to Pyongyang in December 1996 in the hope of a sale to North Korea's state airline Choson Minhang (today Air Koryo).

Another Pratt & Whitney-powered variant was in the works – the Il-96T, a freighter version of the Il-96M. The prototype was RA-96101 and rolled out on April 26, 1997. The Il-96T made its first flight on May 16 and on June 15 it went to Le Bourget for the 1997 Paris Air Show, followed by MAKS-97 in August.

However bigger obstacles were ahead for the Il-96M. The fact is that, ultimately, no matter what euphoria was in the air as both sides of the Cold War enjoyed the peace dividend, Russia and the USA were still competing nations even if their guiding political ideology was now aligned. The US aircraft manufacturers correctly identified an optimised Il-96 with the right engines and the right cockpit as a true competitor for their own products such as the Boeing 777 and McDonnell Douglas MD-11.

Under pressure, the US Export-Import Bank had to add preconditions to financing (such as that Russian airlines would order a certain number of US-made jetliners) but ultimately the contradictions inherent in competitors trying to launch a joint venture meant that talks on financing for future engine and avionics sales were suspended, and the project, dreamed of by the Ilyushin OKB since the dawn of the 1970s, having come so close to fruition, had to be abandoned. In 2001, the PW2337s were taken from the wings of the test machines and replaced by PS-90As.

Some efforts to sustain the project have continued to the present day; Cubana placed an order for the three production Il-96-400Ts to be refurbished to become passenger liners, but thus far they have not materialised. The Russian military has ordered a pair of Il-96-400TZ tankers that will have the capability to dispense up to 65 tons of fuel inflight have a better chance of being delivered, but there is little doubt that at this late stage, they will be the last Il-96s built, and the Soviet widebody product line is at an end. Three production Il-96-400Ts aircraft were built in 2007 and flown for several years by Russian cargo outfit Polet Flight.

Towards the end of 2013, Aeroflot was preparing to stand down its last Soviet airliner as the Il-96 was relegated to leisure trips to Antalya, Larnaca and Tashkent. The last long haul destination was Goa. In the early months of 2014, the last destination with daily Il-96 service was Istanbul, with aviation enthusiasts onboard every flight. The last sortie operated on March 30 with RA-96008. The era of Soviet metal flying in Aeroflot colours was over.

This left just Cubana with Il-96 service, with a secondhand machine taking the fleet up to four frames in August 2015 (RA-96008, Aeroflot's only ship to find a secondhand owner, now CU-T1717). Cubana flew their Il-96 flagships to Madrid and Paris, and to Caracas and Sao Paolo, but at the time of writing, Il-96 flying is sporadic and often substituted by leased-in hardware. The Il-96 flies on in a couple of military roles, as Russia's head of state transport, and as a freighter.

Admittedly the number of airframes produced was small - 106 Il-86s and 30 Il-96s - but the Soviet widebody aircraft were notable because despite being born during times of economic hardship and political turmoil, they were good planes. From an economic standpoint they were effective people movers, and were the visible face of the airline at its most far-flung ports throughout the 90s – New York, Sao Paolo, Singapore, Tokyo, Delhi, London, San Francisco, and more all saw daily Il-96s. (And not a single passenger was lost in an accident.) The Soviet era of airliners remained up-to-date and in frontline international service for a quarter of a century after the Soviet Union itself melted away, a impressive legacy for one of aviation's biggest engineering enterprises.

Polet's hard working Il-96-400T RA-96103 drops into Liège, September 7, 2010 **Guy Viselé**

Pratt & Whitney powered Il-96-400T shows off its long lines in 2008 **Pavel Novikov** Transport-Photo Images

Il-96-400VPU of the FSB **Artyom Kuzhlev**

Fyodor Borisov Transport-Photo Images

Tupolev Tu-204 & -214
The bridge to the future

Various configurations and various missions were considered by the Tupolev OKB for the follow-up to their biggest hit, the Tu-154. In the mid 1970s various widebody options were proposed, one of which bore a striking resemblance to the Lockheed L-1011 Tristar; this was the first use of the Tu-204 designation.

Leonid L. Selyakov was appointed to the head of the programme in January 1979. He pushed the Solviev engine plant to produce a more powerful D-90 turbofan so the Tu-204 widebody could be a twin; assuming a straightforward development programme, this would have started a race against the Boeing 767 to be the world's second widebody twin after the Airbus A300.

To begin work on a replacement for the Tu-154, the Soviet Council of Ministers issued directive no. 782-230 on August 11, 1981. By now the latest Boeing products, the 757 and 767, endorsed Airbus Industrie's vision — the future had just two engines. The Soviet Union's Minister Of The Aircraft Industry, Ivan S. Silayev, demanded that a similar machine be produced in the Soviet Union, with half the fuel consumption of the Tu-154 combined with the most sophisticated systems, avionics, communications equipment and flight computers. Silayev insisted on retaining the original Tu-204 widebody fuselage as did Tu-204 programme head Selyakov, but design bureau founder and head Alexi A. Tupolev held out for a narrowbody design. Tupolev won the argument and Selyakov stood down in disgust, to be replaced by Lev A. Lanovski who took on most of the responsibility for the programme for its entire life, from this process of conception, through design, testing and delivery.

The Soloviev OKB was hard at work creating a new engine, a true high-bypass turbofan which would be the equal of similar powerplants in the West, such as the Pratt & Whitney JT9D, the General Electric CF6 and Rolls-Royce RB211. The Ilyushin OKB was in the midst of updating their short- and medium-haul widebody Il-86 peoplemover to create the Il-96, and were similarly keen to source such an engine. The D-90, later known as the PS-90A, halved fuel burn, noise, and exhaust emissions over previous, 1960s-vintage Soviet jet engines, and it was this powerplant that made the Tu-204 twin a reality.

A second directive from the Soviet Council of Ministers followed on January 18, 1986 which enshrined the narrowbody twin configuration, with an intended first flight for 1988 and an entry into service in the early 1990s. The factory chosen for production was the Ulyanovsk Aircraft Corporation (today the CJSC Aviastar joint venture), 900 kilometres (555 miles) east of Moscow on the Don River, up until that time best known for producing the Antonov An-124 Ruslan super transporter.

An early Tu-204 is on show at the 1991 Paris Air Show — **Pete Hatzakos**

Tu-204s on the factory floor at Aviastar in Ulyanovsk — **Leonid Faerberg** Transport-Photo Images

The high-aspect ratio wing incorporated a supercritical upper surface to reduce drag caused by the build-up of transonic shock waves and was designed in co-operation with TsAGI, the Central Aerohydrodynamic Institute in Moscow. The design of wingtips, engine pylons and the fuselage-wing join were all refined to minimise drag. The proliferation of aerials, sensors, pitot heads and other protrusions was reduced to a minimum, or where unavoidable, their aerodynamic shape was optimised for flight. A system was added to the design to pump fuel from the wing tanks to the vertical stabiliser to move the centre of gravity aft, reducing loading (and hence drag) on the horizontal stabiliser and the fuselage itself (the fuel was pumped back into the wing tanks during descent).

Wide use was made of the latest lightweight aluminium alloys and composites – the use of non-metallic material in the aircraft structure and interior architecture ultimately ended up saving 1,200 kilograms (2,646 lbs). Use of longer lengths of milled and semi-finished sheets of metal meant skin joints were minimised on the fuselage and done away with altogether on the wings, reducing drag as well as structural weight.

The most significant departure from the past was beneath the skin. The Tu-204 was at the cutting edge of fly-by-wire flight controls (where physical linkages from the cockpit to the control surfaces on the wings and tail are done away with in favour of wiring carrying electrical signals attenuated along the way via sophisticated computer software), at the time only previously used on the game-changing Airbus A320 and Concorde. The flight controls themselves were new for a Soviet liner at the time – minimum-movement Y shaped yokes, in a style known as a 'rams horn', most memorably found on Concorde and modern Embraer jets. FADEC (Full Authority Digital Engine Control) for the PS-90A engines was a similarly large leap.

This degree of automation and computerisation in the cockpit reduced the need for a flight engineer to be added to the two pilots (captain and first officer). The reigning political ideology of Soviet Union placed a greater emphasis on creating jobs (even better if they were in the high tech and prestigious field of aviation) than keeping crew costs low, so a role was carved into the operating procedures for a third pilot, who operated facing forwards, manipulating controls mostly on the overhead panel and the centre console. One traditional element of the flight engineer's role, especially on Soviet aircraft, was to operate the throttles, but on the Tu-204, in most flight regimes they were automated.

The two prototypes were CCCP-64001 and a static test frame, built at Tupolev's ANTK experimental plant in Moscow. In the same exact way as the first Tu-104 back in 1955 and many times since, the machine was powered up for systems checks and taxi runs, then disassembled and trucked to Zhukovsky for reassembly in preparation for its first flight. The crew selected for test flying the new bird came under the command of Merited Test Pilot A. I. Talalakin, and included first officer Test Pilot First Class V. N. Matveyev, flight engineers Test Engineer First Class V. V. Solomartin and Test Engineer First Class M. V. Pankevich, and Merited Test Navigator A. N. Nikolaev.

This crew took CCCP-64001 into the cold winter sky first time on at 1248 local time on January 2, 1989 for a successful sortie lasting 32 minutes. The test flying programme for Soviet jetliners traditionally were in two sections – manufacturer's trials to iron out any bugs and confirm (or revise) performance predictions, followed by state trials for type certification. For the Tu-204 it was decided to combine the two phases since the state trials duplicated the factory tests.

This was partly driven by the need to cut costs in the programme, as the Tu-204 was being born in the most turbulent times the Soviet aviation industry had faced since World War 2, as

RA-64008 was with the Tupolev design bureau in the 1990s and scrapped in 1998 by Vnukovo Airlines   **Tom Singfield**

Tu-204 CCCP-64006 was the testbed for the use of Rolls-Royce RB211 engines, Farnborough 1992   **Guy Viselé**

This Tu-204-120CE went on to the China Flight Test Establishment in Xian   **Leonid Faerberg** Transport-Photo Images

the Soviet Union itself was about to blow apart under the weight of the sclerotic economic system with all its inbuilt contradictions and restrictions. It is testament to the perseverance of the Tupolev team and the factory workers in Ulyanovsk that with their country changing radically around them, they were able to stay on course with their ambitious new aircraft.

CCCP-64003, -64004 and -64006 were used in the test programme which incorporated sales trips to perform aerobatic displays at both Farnborough and Paris as well as to potential export markets as Iran, India, the United Arab Emirates and Thailand. One airframe was lent to Vnukovo Airlines on March 25 1993 for service trials involving ground crew and the training of pilots. Cargo runs out of the airline's eponymous Moscow base carried commercial cargo to the newly-renamed Saint Petersburg (previously Leningrad), plus Volgograd, Irkutsk, Ekaterinburg, Mineral'nyye Vody, Norilsk and Omsk, and on international cargo flights to Almaty (previously Alma-Ata), Bishkek, Kiev and Tashkent. These trials ended on December 20, by which time flight testing was complete and the preliminary test protocol was signed three days later.

Bureaucratic hurdles under the new Russian regime slowed down the final certification which took a whole year to come through in December 1994, issued by the CIS Interstate Aviation Committee. Back in 1992 a state programme had called for a national fleet of 145 long haul Il-96s and no less than 530 Tu-204s; alas by the middle of the decade, with the new Russian republic struggling to get back on its feet after the upheaval of the end of the Soviet Union, times were tough, and the resources for such a huge aircraft replacement programme had evaporated. Unbowed, Russia introduced its latest jetliner into revenue service on February 23, 1996 when Vnukovo Airines operated RA-64011 on a scheduled flight from Moscow Vnukovo to Mineral'nyye Vody.

After the first 15 aircraft were rolled out at Aviastar, the Tu-204-100 was created, with a maximum takeoff weight raised to 94.6 tons (189,200 pounds) and range increased to 5,000 kilometres (3,107 miles).

The next evolution was more significant. For the first time since the Mikoyan MiG-15 of the early 1950s, a Russian-built craft was powered by a Rolls-Royce engine, with the Tu-204 being suitably sophisticated to be compatible with the

A Rolls-Royce powered Tu-204-120 of Air Cairo, flying for Mahan Air of Iran   Konstantin von Wedelstaedt

■ Aviastar operate this Tu-204-100C freighter in the stunning livery of Russia Post   **Artyom Kuzhlev**

■ Cubana's Tu-204-100CE freigher parachutes into Quito, March 20, 2010. At one point Cubana had four active Tu-204s including two passenger machines   **Andres Ramirez**

Rolls-Royce RB.211 engine more usually found on the Lockheed L-1011 Tristar and some Boeing 747s, 757s and 767s. It also took the political environment to become sufficiently peaceful to enable such an exchange of technology. The traditional second-wind designation of Tu-204M was dropped in favour of Tu-204-120.

Tu-204 CCCP-64004 was re-engined with Rollers and took to the air for the first time as a Tu-204-120 in August 1992; the first production model was RA-64027 and was flown for the first time on March 6, 1997. In 1998 Sirocco Aerospace brokered a deal for two Tu-204-120s to be placed with Air Cairo. RA-64027 became SU-EAF and -64028 became SU-EAG. The pair were delivered to Egypt on November 11 followed by a third machine, SU-EAH, which was delivered to its new home on January 24, 1999.

A new round of upgrades to the Tu-204 started with an initiative by the Kazan Aircraft Production Association, known as KAPO, to build additional airframes themselves. KAPO, like Aviastar, had a significant amount of control over the design of the variant they were producing, independent of the Tupolev OKB. The differences made by KAPO when they began producing their own machines were sufficient to create a new aircraft type, the Tu-214. The main visible difference is the number two exit, just forward of the leading edge of the wing, was enlarged to be a full-size type I entrance door. Under the skin were two extra fuel tanks and the structural enhancements to cope with the increased gross weight. The first Tu-214 flew on March 21, 1996.

The Tu-214's extra range and payload capacity made it the Russian state's choice over the Tu-204 to be the platform for all special mission variants. Today only a handful are in passenger service, but government and military airframes fly across Russia daily on a number of specialised missions. The Tu-214ON is a geological surveyor fitted with panoramic, topographic, thermographic and aerial cameras as well as side-looking radar. Two such airframes are in service: RA-64519 flew first, on June 1, 2011, followed by RA-64525 on December 18, 2013, replacing Tu-154s and An-30s in similar roles.

■ RA-64008 had a brief stint in 2008 in an unusual billboard livery **Yury Kirsanov** Transport-Photo Images

■ Tu-204-100S RA-64021 was damaged beyond repair in a hard landing at Norilsk on August 24, 2016 **Guy Viselé**

■ RA-64001 Tu-234 after retirement at Zhukovsky **Aeroprints dot com**

■ Tu-214 RA-64501 operated by KAPO, the factory airline, and seen at the 1996 Farnborough airshow **Tom Singfield**

The Russian Ministry of Defence operate two Tu-214PU airborne command posts and two Tu-214SUS communications relay platforms; the government has a pair of Tu-204SR machines in the same role. The Ministry of Defence have a pair of top-secret Tu-214R ELINT (electronic signals intelligence) aircraft fitted with a maze of electronic, signals and communications intelligence-gathering receptors including sideways-looking SAR (Synthetic Aperture Radar).

It was intended that the Tu-204 would provide a starting point for a range of new airliners, in the way the contemporary Airbus A320 gave rise to the stretched A321 and the smaller A319 and A318. The Tu-204 was thus shrunk to create a short body version, the Tu-204-300 which was also known at the Tupolev OKB as the Tu-234. With a shorter, and hence lighter fuselage, but the same wing, engines, and fuel tankage, the -300 was a special performance variant with range extended to 9,000 kilometres (5,592 miles) and the ability to get airborne from short runways and unreinforced concrete surfaces.

As early as 1994 the prototype RA-64001 was converted to become a non-flying Tu-204-300 demonstrator, but it wasn't until August 16, 2003 that RA-64026, the true Tu-204-300 prototype, made its first flight. It had its public unveiling the very same day by performing a fly-by at the MAKS 2003 air show at Zhukovsky airfield. The first production Tu-204-300 was handed over to Vladivostok Avia on May 20, 2005, and went into revenue service on June 27. Vnukovo Airlines took a total of five, and Rossiya, an arm of the Russian government, took four. One became a VIP machine.

Despite two factories building the high tech Tupolev, there were very few domestic buyers due to the extremely low level of available cash in Russia. There were hundreds of middle-aged Soviet-era airliners in service, plus the Tu-154 and Il-62 were still in production as late as the mid-1990s, so there was no shortage of existing capacity, some with very low airframe hours. Even the old bangers, Tu-154Bs, Il-62 non-Ms and Tu-134s, were reasonably

These two Tu-204-300s served Vladivostok Avia from June 2005 until October 2013   **Leonid Faerberg** Transport-Photo Images

Front office of a Rossiya Tu-204-300
Alexander Mishin Transport-Photo Images

Overhead panel on a Rossiya Tu-204-300
Alexander Mishin Transport-Photo Images

viable as acquisition price was negligible, fuel was cheap and passenger expectations were low.

International sales were equally challenging – despite the very cheap purchase price of a new Tupolev compared to the latest Airbus and Boeing, airlines rely on a global network of spare parts availability, multi-lingual tech support, and local engineering know-how to keep their fleets flying, and Tupolev could not provide that essential web of support outside of their own geopolitical sphere.

Despite these hurdles, Aviastar and KAPO were able to sustain production and place aircraft with airlines for a couple of decades, albeit at the incredibly low level of, in some years, one single aircraft annually (1990, 1995, 1998 and 2014) and only two in others (1991, 1992, 1994, 1999, 2004, and 2007). Russian leisure carrier Transero operated five over the years; Kras Air had up to six flying out of their hometown of Krasnoyarsk, Dalavia had five at their far eastern base at Khabarovsk; and Aviastar, an airline started up by the factory to soak up some of the unsold planes parked on their ramp at Ulyanovsk, employed several. KAPO had their own airline too, flying both Ulyanovsk-built Tu-204s and their own Tu-214s on charter and cargo flights in Russia and abroad.

Gradually, export customers were found, such as as Iran's biggest private airline, Mahan Air, who leased two of Cairo Aviation's Tu-204-120s, SU-EAI and -EAF, repainted in Mahan's smart white and green livery and operated mostly on the busy route to Dubai, starting in October 2005 and flying up until the end of the contract in December 2006. SU-EAI returned to Iran for another three months of flying starting in March 2007.

A unique Tu-204-300 became an export success story. The twelfth Tu-204 *sans suffixe* to roll off the line at Ulyanovsk (in retrospect, it could be considered an early Tu-204-100) was returned by Vnukovo Airlines at the time the Tu-204-300 programme was beginning. Two barrels of fuselage were chopped out and the remainder was put back together, creating what was effectively a new Tu-204-300 (indeed, the airframe hours were reset to zero). This machine became P-632, the first Tu-204

Five Red Wings Tu-204s line up at Domodedovo **Alexander Mishin** Transport-Photo Images

Air Koryo's hand-made Tu-204-300 resting on the ramp at Pyongyang   Simon De Rudder

to be delivered to North Korea's national carrier Air Koryo, touching down at their Pyongyang base on Christmas Eve 2007. A regular Tu-204-100B followed on January 17, 2010; both aircraft remain in service as North Korea's flagships.

The other country to remain firmly wedded to command economy socialism after the demise of the Soviet Union was Cuba, and Cubana took delivery of three Tu-204-100s in 2007, led by CU-C1700 which arrived in Havana for the first time on September 4, followed by CU-C1701 and CU-C1702 both on December 28. CU-C1703 joined the tropical fun just over a year later, on February 17, 2009. One remains in service today, with three in long term storage at Havana.

Despite these victories, the Tu-204 export narrative was dogged by the sales that fell through — a widely-trumpeted order by Air Zimbabwe failed to materialise, and around the time of the Mahan Air lease, a combined Iran order for 40 machines across Iran Air Tour, Caspian Airlines and Kish Air was announced. The logic went something like, the Tu-204 could find a niche with airlines who are unable to buy new Western equipment due to diplomatic rows with the United States or the European Union. In reality even the PS-90A powered Tu-204s contained plenty of Western avionics such as the Honeywell navigation suite, Allied-Signal or Collins TCAS, and Litton integrated GPS, and the PS-90As themselves contained elements developed in partnership with Pratt & Whitney. So export sales to sanctioned nations would certainly have been a headache but in any case a country like Iran with a mature airline scene would probably struggle if it operated a large fleet of an aircraft type that came with only the limited customer support Tupolev could provide. Whether it was politics or operational issues that were the hurdle, the big Iranian order was just like all the rest — a mirage.

Despite such disheartening sales, the factory at Ulyanovsk kept working on their machine, producing an update called the Tu-204SM, spurred on in part by the superior capability of KAPO's Tu-214. It utilised the uprated PS-90A2 engine, improved avionics, a new APU, enhanced climate control in the passenger cabin, a certified payload increase from 21 tons (46,297 pounds) to 23 tons (50,706 pounds), a range of 4,500 kilometres (2,800 miles) and a true two-crew operation, dispensing

■ This Tu-204-100B was delivered new to Red Wings in September 2008 — **Artyom Kuzhlev**

■ The comfortable passenger interior of RA-64046, a Red Wings Tu-204-100B, flying from Moscow to Simferopol June 28, 2015
Simon De Rudder

with the role of flight engineer. Prototype RA-64150 first flew on December 29, 2010, with initial deliveries to Red Wings planned for 2011. A lack of orders meant the prototype remains the only Tu-204SM to exist, and is in sporadic service with the Ulyanovsk factory as a multi-purpose aircraft, with duties including starring in a Russian movie, *The Crew 2*, in 2014.

Two have been lost in accidents, but luckily neither had passengers onboard – the first incident, in 2010, saw factory-owned Aviastar 1906 come down short of the runway at Moscow Domodedovo airport at the conclusion of a ferry flight from Hurghada in Egypt due to pilot error without any fatalities; on December 29, 2012, Red Wings 9268 overran runway 32 at Moscow Vnukovo at the end of a ferry flight from Pardubice in the Czech Republic when a software logic failure caused the engines to produced full forward thrust instead of reverse, and five of the eight crew onboard lost their lives. Despite these two incidents, the Tu-204 has proved itself to be safe and reliable in service.

The story of the Tu-204 is the story of optimism in the midst of trial. The solar system of socialist economies that orbited Russia from the end of World War Two up to the end of the 1980s, with a somewhat captive market of nations and their airlines, not to mention a gigantic local carrier that would guarantee hundreds of orders, was gone. While the Tu-204 was impressively hi tech, with bearable economics, it simply couldn't get a foot in the door with the mass-market behemoths of Boeing and Airbus able to provide on-the-spot tech support and spares supplies at almost any airport on the planet, sophisticated fly-now-pay-later financing for even the smallest carrier backed by the thriving modern national economies in Europe and the United States; and the A320s and 737s, having grown up in a more politically stable environment, represented a more evolved product too.

The Tu-204 and -214 are current product lines, although the reality is that the only possible customer would be the Russian military, and for them any of the 26 mostly low-hour airframes that are in storage would suffice, which includes nine of their preferred Tu-214. That leaves 25 Tu-204s and 15 military Tu-214s currently flying. The biggest airline operator is Red Wings with eight, although retirement plans are in place. Air Koryo still fly their pair of Tu-204s, a standard -100B and their rare abbreviated custom shop -300. The China Flight Test Establishment have a sole Tu-204-120 that was originally delivered to Air China Cargo.

In fact with only 63 of all variants built over a 26 year period, the Tu-204 could, on first glance, be considered a dud. However what is worth considering is that this machine was born in the middle of a revolution and built against a backdrop of ongoing political upheaval as Russia, freshly-shorn of its empire, tried to find its feet. Not only was production sustained, but the aircraft itself is as efficient and safe as any contemporary Western product, and its lack of commercial success is more down to the inability to ramp up production and the inability to provide global technical support – all a function of events far beyond Tupolev's control.

Since Russia has found most of its way back to stability and wealth in recent years, the aerospace industry has at last begun to recapture some of the glory of its youth, with 159 Sukhoi Superjet 100 commuter jetliners already produced and placed in service with a wide range of airlines, and the Irkut MC-21 mainline narrowbody jetliner test flying, promising to be a viable competitor to the Airbus A320 and Boeing 737 family. These advanced aircraft for the twenty-first century wouldn't be possible if the Russian aerospace industry had withered away, and so the Tu-204 can rightly be seen as an essential bridge through the difficult post-Soviet years to the present day.

B. Korzin Transport-Photo Images

- Source: Official Airline Guide (OAG) January 1986 edition (via Routes Online)

  Key (ABC World Airways Guide/OAG standard):
  TU3 Tupolev Tu-134; **TU5** Tupolev Tu-154; **IL6** Ilyushin Il-62; **ILW** Ilyushin Il-86; **IL8** Ilyushin Il-18; **AN4** Antonov An-24
  Local flights (eg Yak-40, AN4) were not published internationally
  The number (Belgrade **3** TU5 SU161/162) refers to the weekly frequency of the flight (in this case, SU161 out to Belgrade and 162 back operated three times per week).

- For brevity, multistop international routes are only listed by their terminus, so some destinations are hidden in the text, such as Bombay, because all of its six weekly flights continued on to other ports – Rangoon, Dhaka, Bangkok, Singapore, Calcutta and Colombo in this case, depending on the day. Aircraft needing to pick up fuel en route heading out to foreign climes or on their way home created a couple of mini hubs. In this timetable, Budapest enjoyed direct same-plane service to Algiers, Bamako, Bissau, Buenos Aires, Casablanca, Conakry, Dakar, Freetown, Luanda, Lusaka, Malta, Marseilles, Monrovia, Nouadhibou, Ouagadougou, Tripoli and Tunis, more international service than Leningrad. Odessa, a charming but small Ukrainian spa town on the shore of the Black Sea found itself with service to Accra, Brazzaville, Cotonou, Douala, Malabo, and Tripoli. Simferopol in the Crimea was another repeat offender, with Abu Dhabi, Aden, Amman, Antananarivo, Bajumbura, Cairo, Djibouti, Dar Es Salaam, Entebbe, Larnaca, Mogadishu, Nairobi, Kigali, Khartoum, Kuwait, Maputo, Seychelles. One final laundry list of destinations – Shannon, on the windswept west coast of Ireland, was on the flight plan en route to Havana, Lima, Kingston, Managua and Mexico City. Quite an impressive transatlantic network for a beautiful but rural and sparsely populated area.

- Aeroflot in the time of the Soviet Union was a totally unique network and for a student of the airline industry, geography or politics, their timetables are worth reading from beginning to end like a spy novel. This was not just an airline, it was also a foreign policy. Happy hunting.

Aeroflot timetable
winter 1985 / 1986

from Moscow SVO international
Accra via Odessa, Tripoli & Cotonou 3 per month TU5 SU417/418
Aden via Simferopol & Cairo 1 TU5 SU449/450
Aleppo via Yerevan fortnightly TU5 SU519/520
Algiers via Budapest 1 TU5 SU407/408
Algiers via Budapest & Tunis 1 TU5 SU409/410
Amsterdam via Warsaw 2 TU5 SU229/230
Antananarivo via Simferopol, Cairo, Aden & Nairobi 1 TU5 SU459/460
Athens via Sofia 2 TU5 SU295/296
Baghdad via Larnaca 1 TU5 SU513/514
Bamako via Budapest, Tripoli & Ouagadougou 3 per month TU5 SU423/424
Bangkok via Bombay 1 IL6 SU551/552 & IL6 SU553/554
Beijing 1 IL6 SU571/572
Belgrade 3 TU5 SU161/162
Berlin SXF 7 ILW SU111/112 & 7 TU5 SU113/114
Bissau via Budapest, Casablanca, & Nouadhibou 1 per month TU5 SU415/416
Bourgas 1 TU3 SU177/178
Bratislava 2 TU3 SU145/146
Brazzaville via Odessa, Tripoli & Douala 1 TU5 SU419/420
Brussels 1 TU5 & 1 TU3 SU231/232
Budapest 5 TU5 & 2 TU3 SU131/132
Bucharest 2 TU5 & 1 TU3 SU151/152
Buenos Aires via Budapest & Dakar 1 IL6 SU351/352
Bujumbura via Simferopol, Cairo & Nairobi monthly TU5 SU445/446
Calcutta via Bombay 1 IL6 SU537/538
Casablanca via Budapest & Malta 1 TU5 SU427/428
Colombo via Bombay 1 IL6 SU545/546
Copenhagen 1 IL6 SU580/579, 1 IL6 SU552/551 & 1 IL6 SU554/553
Copenhagen via Stockholm 1 IL6 SU217/218
Delhi via Tashkent 1 ILW SU535/536
Dhaka via Tashkent, Karachi & Bombay 1 TU5 SU549/550
Dresden 6 TU3 SU119/120
Dresden via Efrurt 3 TU3 SU123/124
Dusseldorf 1 TU3 SU201/202
Frankfurt 1 IL6 SU259/260, 3 TU3 & 3 TU5 SU255/256
Geneva 1 TU5 SU271/272
Hanoi via Tashkent, Karachi & Calcutta 2 ILW SU541/542
Havana via Shannon & Gander 3 ILW SU333/334
Helsinki 4 TU5 SU203/204 & 2 TU3 SU205/206
Kabul via Tashkent 1 TU5 SU531/532
Khartoum via Simferopol & Cairo monthly TU5 SU431/432
Kigali via Simferopol, Cairo, Nairobi & Entebbe monthly TU5 SU445/446
Kingston via Shannon & Havana 1 IL6 SU331/332
Lagos via Vienna & Tripoli 1 TU5 SU421/422 & 1 TU5 SU425/426
Leipzig 3 TU3 SU121/122
Lima via Luxembourg, Shannon & Havana 1 IL6 SU335/336 & 1 IL6 SU343/344
Lisbon via Prague 2 TU3 SU235/236
London Heathrow 1 IL6 SU243/244, 2 IL6 SU241/242 & 2 IL6 SU582/581

■ Domodedovo airport in the mid 1980s; eight Tu-154s, two Il-62s, an Il-86 and a Tu-134

Valentin Grebnev Transport-Photo Images

■ The unmistakable thumbprint of a Tu-134

Artyom Kuzhlev

Longyearbyen via Murmansk 1-2 per month TU5 SU207/208
Luanda via Budapest 2 IL6 SU433/434
Lusaka via Budapest & Luanda 1 IL6 SU435/436
Luxembourg via Leningrad 1 TU3 SU233/234
Madrid via Berlin SXF 1 TU5 SU299/300
Managua via Shannon & Havana 1 IL6 SU339/340
Maputo via Simferopol, Cairo, Djibouti & Dar es Salaam 1 TU5 SU453/454
Marseille via Budapest 1 TU3 SU287/288
Mexico City via Shannon & Havana 1 IL6 SU341/342
Milan MXP 2 TU5 SU285/286
Monrovia via Budapest, Tripoli & Bamako monthly TU5 SU423/424
Montreal 1 IL6 SU301/302
Munich 1 TU3 SU257/258
Nairobi via Simferopol & Cairo fortnightly TU5 SU445/446
Oslo via Stockholm 2 TU5 SU211/212
Paris CDG 1 IL6 SU253/254, 1 IL6 SU576/575, 1 IL6 & 4 TU5 SU251/252
Prague 7 TU5 SU141/142
Pyongyang 1 IL6 SU567/568
Rome 1 IL6 SU283/284, 1 TU5 SU281/282, & 1 IL6 SU584/583
Singapore via Bombay 1 IL6 SU559/560
Singapore via Delhi 2 IL6 SU557/558
Sofia 5 TU5 SU171/172
Tehran 1 IL6 SU515/516
Tokyo (8 weekly total)
1 IL6 SU575/576, 1 IL6 SU577/578, 1 IL6 SU579/580, 2 IL6 SU581/582, 1 IL6 SU583/584, 1 IL6 SU585/586, & 1 IL6 SU587/588
Ulaan Baatar via Omsk & Irkutsk 2 TU3 & 1 TU5 5SU561/562
Varna 1 TU3 SU175/176
Vienna 2 TU5 SU261/262, 3 TU3 & 1 IL6 SU263/264
Vientiane via Tashkent, Karachi, Bombay & Rangoon 1 TU5 SU533/534
Warsaw 2 TU5 5 SU101/102
Zurich 2 TU5 SU265/266
Zagreb via Kiev 1 TU5 SU165/166

triangle routings ex-SVO
SVO - Leningrad - Shannon - SVO 1 TU3 SU247/248
SVO - Odessa - Tripoli - Cotonou - Malabo - Accra - Cotonou - Tripoli - Odessa - SVO monthly TU5 SU417/418
SVO - Simferopol - Cairo - Addis Ababa - Aden - Cairo - Simferopol - SVO 1 TU5 SU455/456
SVO - Simferopol - Cairo - Aden - Dar es Salaam - Mogadishu - Aden - Cairo - Simferopol - SVO 3 per month TU5 SU447/448
SVO - Simferopol - Cairo - Aden - Dar es Salaam - Seychelles - Aden - Cairo - Simferopol - SVO monthly TU5 SU447/448
SVO - Simferopol - Cairo - Sana'a - Djibouti - Cairo - Simferpol - SVO 1 TU5 SU451/452
SVO - Cairo - Simferopol - SVO fortnightly TU5 SU441/442
SVO - Dakar - Conakry - Budapest - SVO 3 per month TU5 SU413/414
SVO - Dakar - Conakry - Dakar - Budapest - SVO 3 per month TU5 SU411/412
SVO - Dakar - Freetown - Dakar - Budapest - SVO monthly IL6 SU411/412
SVO - Sal - Dakar - Conakry - Dakar - Budapest - SVO monthly TU5 SU413/414
SVO - Beirut - Larnaca - SVO 1 TU5 SU509/510
SVO - Damascus - Larnaca - SVO 2 TU5 SU517/518
SVO - Istanbul - Ankara - SVO 1 TU3 SU501/502
SVO - Simferopol - Larnaca - Amman - Larnaca - SVO 1 TU3 SU505/506
SVO - Simeropol - Larnaca - Kuwait - Abu Dhabi - Larnaca - SVO 1 TU5 SU521/522
SVO - Bombay - Hanoi - Bombay - Mineralnye Vody - SVO 1 IL6 SU541/542
SVO - Bombay - Hanoi - Phnom Penh - Saigon - Bombay - SVO fortnightly IL6 SU573/574
SVO - Delhi - Kuala Lumpur - Delhi - Tashkent - SVO 1 IL6 SU547/548
SVO - Karachi - Colombo - Karachi - Tashkent - SVO 1 IL6 SU543/544
SVO - Karachi - Kuala Lumpur - Karachi - Tashkent - SVO 1 IL6 SU555/556
SVO - Novosibirsk - Ulaan Baatar - Irkutsk - Omsk - SVO 1 TU5 SU563/564
SVO - Tashkent - Karachi - Calcutta - Hanoi - Saigon - Calcutta - Karachi - Tashkent - SVO fortnightly ILW SU569/570
SVO - Gander - Havana - Lima - Havana - Shannon - SVO 1 IL6 SU345/346 & 1 IL6 SU347/348

from Moscow SVO domestic
Leningrad shuttle
7 TU5 SU2435/2436
7 TU3 SU2417/2418
7 TU3 SU2415/2416
5 TU5 SU2419/2420
7 TU3 SU2429/2430
Minsk 7 TU3 SU1983/1984
Irkutsk via Omsk 2 IL6 SU561/562
Riga 7 TU5 SU2085/2086 & 7 TU5 SU2093/2094
Tallinn 7 TU3 SU2113/2114
Vilnius 7 TU3 SU2017/2018

from Moscow DME
Alma Ata 7 ILW SU1505/1506
Baku 7 TU5 SU859/860 & 7 TU5 SU861/862
Dushanbe 7 TU5 SU1631/1632
Yerevan 7 SU897/898 TU5 & 7 TU5 SU893/894
Tashkent 7 ILW SU1661/1662
Urgench 3 TU5 SU2693/2694
Volgograd 7 TU3 SU1301/1302
DME – Batumi – Sukhumi – DME 7 IL8 SU971/972

from Moscow VKO
Adler/Sochi 7 TU5 SU1017/1018
Kharkov 7 TU3 SU1489/1490
Kiev 7 TU5 SU1767/1768 & 7 TU5 SU1769/1770
Kishinev 7 TU3 SU1741/1742
Krasnodar 7 TU5 SU1137/1138
Odessa 7 TU5 SU1687/1688 & 7 TU5 SU1697/1698
Rostov 7 TU5 SU1171/1172
Samarkand 4 TU5 SU1685/1686 & 7 TU5 SU2687/2688
Simferopol 7 ILW SU1589/1590
Tbilisi 7 TU5 SU923/924 & 7 TU5 SU935/936

from Leningrad international
Amsterdam 1 TU3 SU633/634
Athens via Berlin Schoenfeld 1 TU3 SU659/660
Berlin SXF 7 TU5 SU609/610
Budapest via Warsaw 2 TU3 SU617/618
Dresden 1 TU5 SU611/612
LED – Erfurt – Dresden – LED 1 TU3 SU613/614
Frankfurt 1 TU3 SU655/656
Hamburg 1 TU3 SU653/654
Helsinki 1 TU3 SU639/640 & 2 TU5 SU645/646
Helsinki 1 TU5 SU641/642 & 2 TU3 SU631/632
Leipzig 2 TU5 SU607/608
London Heathrow 1 IL6 SU637/638
Paris CDG 1 ILW SU643/644
Prague 2 TU5 SU621/622
Oslo via Stockholm 1 TU3 SU635/636
Tampere 1 TU5 SU651/652
Zurich via Vienna 1 TU5 SU657/658

from Leningrad domestic
Adler/Sochi 2 TU5 SU8591/SU8592,
7 ILW SU8583/8584 & 2 TU5 SU8589/8590
Baku 7 TU5 SU6709/6710
Yerevan 6 TU5 SU7216/7215
Khabarovsk 5 IL6 SU3832/3831
Kiev 7 TU5 SU8643/8644
Kishinev 7 TU3 SU7632/7631
Krasnodar 3 TU3 SU8569/8570
Lviv 7 Tu134 SU8677/8678
Mineralnye Vody 4 TU5 SU8559/8560
Minsk 7 TU3 SU7842/7841
Odessa 7 TU5 SU8657/8658
Rostov 7 TU5 SU6110/6109
Simferopol 6 TU5 SU8611/8612

Tashkent 7 IL6 SU5060/5059
Tbilisi 7 TU5 SU6882/6881
Vilnius 3 TU3 SU8046/8045
Volgograd 6 TU3 SU8547/8548 & 4 TU3 SU8549/8550

from Kiev international
Belgrade 1 TU3 SU687/688
Berlin SXF 2 TU3 SU665/666
Dusseldorf 1 TU3 SU673/674
Paris CDG 1 TU3 SU699/700
Sofia 1 TU3 SU685/686 & 1 TU3 SU669/670

from Kiev domestic
Adler/Sochi 3 TU5 SU7301/7302
Baku 5 TU5 SU6684/6683
Yerevan 7 TU5 SU7194/7193
Mineralnye Vody 5 TU5 SU6368/6367
Simferopol 2 TU5 SU7359/7360
Tashkent 7 IL6 SU5042/5041
Tbilisi 7 TU5 SU7287/7288

from Simferopol international
Berlin SXF 1 TU5 SU855/856
Dresden 2 TU5 SU881/882
Leipzig 3 TU5 SU879/880
Prague 2 per month TU5 SU825/826

from Minsk
Adler/Sochi 7 TU3 SU7791/7792
Odessa 6 TU3 SU7823/7824

from Adler/Sochi international
Berlin SXF 1 TU5 SU871/872
Budapest 1 TU5 SU853/854
Dresden 2 TU5 SU873/874
Leipzig 4 TU5 SU877/878
Prague 5-6 per month TU5 SU823/824

from Tashkent
Alma Ata 7 IL6 SU4993/4994
Irkutsk via Alma Ata 5 TU5 SU3720/3719
Frunze (now Bishkek) 7 TU3 SU4680/4679
Khabarovsk 5 IL6 SU4935/4936
Tbilisi 7 TU5 SU6816/6815
Urgench 4 TU5 SU5079/5080
Urgench via Mineralnye Vody 4 TU3 SU4999/5000

non hub routes
Khabarovsk – Niigata 1 TU5 SU695/696
Khabarovsk – Pyongyang 1 IL8 SU697/698
Yerevan – Beirut – Larnaca – Yerevan 1 TU5 SU511/512
Yerevan – Baku 7 TU3 SU6644/6643
& 7 TU3 SU6646/6645
Vilnius – Riga – Tallinn 5 AN4 SU8081/8082
Minsk – Berlin SXF 2 TU3 SU691/692

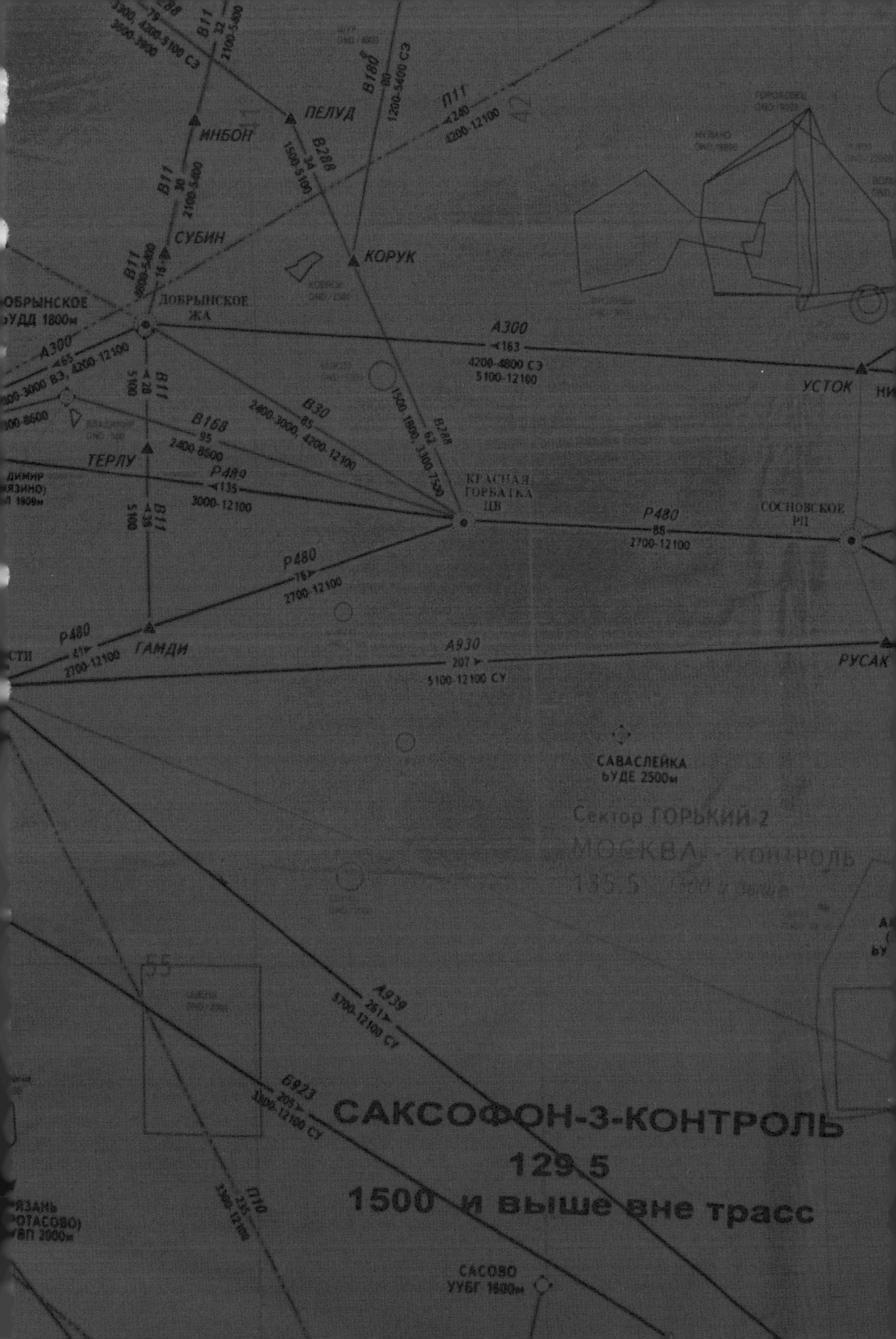

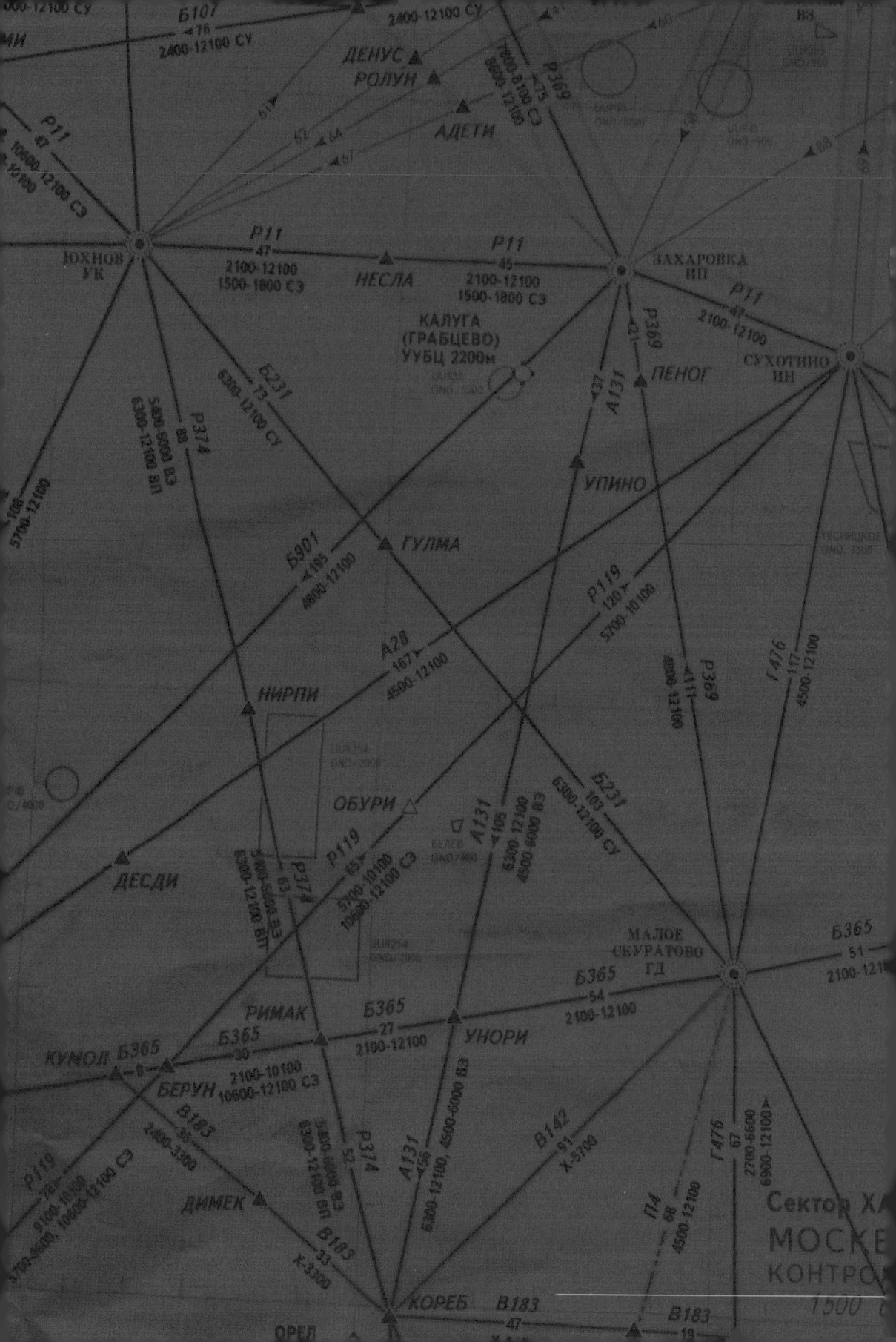